The sixth book in the Master Comprehension series helps children to read and comprehend detailed information. Facts about sports, dinosaurs, poetry, music, photography and other high-interest topics are presented in an entertaining and highly readable style. In addition to skills presented in previous books, students learn in this book to identify generalizations and to recognize and make comparisons. The 8 skills covered in this book are listed in the Glossary.

## Table of Contents

# Glossary

**Comparison.** A way to recognize or show how things are alike or different.

**Comprehension.** Understanding what is seen, heard or read.

**Context.** A way to figure out the meaning of a new word by relating it to the other words in the sentence.

**Fact.** A fact can be proved.

**Following Directions.** Doing what the directions say to do.

**Generalization.** A generalization is a statement or principle that applies in many different situations.

**Main Idea.** Finding the most important points.

**Opinion.** An opinion, which cannot be proved, tells what someone believes.

**Recognizing Details.** Being able to pick out and remember the who, what, when, where, why and how of what is read.

Name: _____

# Comparing Notes On Field Hockey

Comparison is a way to recognize how things are alike or different.

**Directions:** Read each paragraph, then answer the questions about making comparisons between field hockey, basketball and softball.

My sister is more interested in sports than I am. Last year she lettered in field hockey, basketball and softball. I got my exercise walking to school.

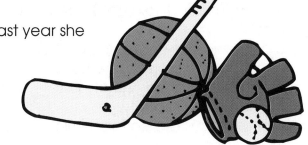

1. What sports did the writer play?

_____

My sister's favorite sport is field hockey. Because it requires constant running up and down a field, it provides more exercise than basketball and softball. There's also more danger, because every year someone gets her teeth knocked out with a hockey stick. So far at our school, no one has lost any teeth to basketball or softball.

2. Compared to basketball and softball, field hockey provides one benefit and one danger. Name them.

_____

On the other hand, softball players—especially those who play the outfield—can occasionally take some time to daydream. With an ace strikeout pitcher and batters who can't hit far, outfielders' gloves don't get much of a workout.

3. What sports **do not** allow time for daydreaming?

_____

Write a short paragraph telling which sport you like best and why.

_____

_____

_____

# Floor Exercises For Gymnasts

Have you ever seen gymnasts perform?  Their grace and strength is beautiful to see!  Good gymnasts make their activities look easy—they never sweat or strain. In reality, it takes enormous strength, agility and flexibility to perform as a gymnast.

At a gymnastics competition, athletes perform these activities:  floor exercises, side horse, rings, long horse, parallel bars and horizontal bar. Among these, floor exercises require the most grace and creativity.

Floor exercises are performed in an area that is 39 feet long by 39 feet wide (12 meters by 12 meters). Each gymnast must stay within these lines. If so much as a toe strays outside the area, the judges deduct points from the gymnast's score.

The performance, called a "routine," usually must last only 50 to 70 seconds. Each gymnast's routine must include certain jumping and tumbling activities, or "stunts." Among these are somersaults, jumps, and backwards and forwards handsprings. Each stunt must appear to flow naturally into the next so that the routine looks like it's "all of a piece" instead of a series of random hops and leaps. Music helps set the pace for each gymnast's routine.  Because each gymnast chooses different music, it also helps to make each routine distinctive.

**Directions:** Answer the questions about gymnastics.

1. Name three skills good gymnasts must possess. 1) _____

2) _____          3) _____

2. How many activities do gymnasts perform at a competition?_____

3. In what size area are floor exercises performed? _____

4. A gymnastic performance is called a

   ☐ stunt   ☐ competition   ☐ routine

5. Which is not part of a floor routine?

   ☐ jumps   ☐ rings   ☐ handsprings

Name: _____

# Fact Or Opinion?

A fact can be proved. An opinion, which cannot be proved, tells what someone believes.

**Directions:** Read the numbered sentences and put an x in the corresponding numbered boxes to tell whether each sentence gives a fact or an opinion.

1. Gymnasts are the most exciting athletes to watch!

1. ☐ Fact ☐ Opinion

2. Because their sport requires all-over body strength, gymnasts must have very strong arms and legs. Their stomach muscles and the muscles in their feet must also be in good condition.

2. ☐ Fact ☐ Opinion

3. To do handstands, gymnasts must support the weight of their upside-down bodies by holding their hands flat and their arms straight. Their legs must be pointed straight up.

3. ☐ Fact ☐ Opinion

4. With a little practice, I think anyone could learn to do a handstand.

4. ☐ Fact ☐ Opinion

5. A somersault is more difficult than a handstand.

5. ☐ Fact ☐ Opinion

6. It requires starting and stopping from a standing position after making a 360-degree turn in the air.

6. ☐ Fact ☐ Opinion

7. I'll bet not many people can do a good somer-sault!

7. ☐ Fact ☐ Opinion

8. Some of the different kinds of somersaults are backwards somersaults, sideways somersaults and something called a "bent body" somersault.

8. ☐ Fact ☐ Opinion

9. I've never seen a bent body somersault, but I think it must require a lot of bending.

9. ☐ Fact ☐ Opinion

10. I don't think I would be any good at the bent body somersault.

10. ☐ Fact ☐ Opinion

# Warming Up To Gymnastics

Because no bats, racquets or balls are used, some people mistakenly believe that gymnastics is not a dangerous sport. Although major injuries don't happen often, broken legs—as well as broken necks and backs—can occur. The reason they don't happen frequently is that gymnasts follow safety rules that help prevent accidents.

One thing gymnasts are careful to do every time they practice their sport is to first warm up their muscles. "Warm-ups" are exercises that gently stretch and loosen the muscles before subjecting them to tension and strain.

Warm-ups help the muscles gradually expand and stretch so they move efficiently during vigorous exercise. Without a warm-up of 15 to 30 minutes it's possible that unworked muscles will be dangerously pulled or strained. Because a muscle injury can interfere with—or stop—an athlete's performance, experienced gymnasts never skip or rush through their warm-ups.

Another thing gymnasts do to help prevent accidents is to use "spotters" when they practice. Spotters are people—usually other gymnasts—who stand beside gymnasts when they are practicing new movements. If gymnasts twist the wrong way or begin to fall, spotters will grab them to prevent injury. Spotters also often offer helpful advice and instant feedback on gymnasts' performances.

**Directions:** Answer the questions about gymnastics.

1. Name two things gymnasts can do to prevent accidents.

1.) _____    2.) _____

2. What's the purpose of a warm-up?

_____

3. Name three things spotters can do to help gymnasts.

1.) _____    2.) _____    3.) _____

4. Which is not a good length of time for gymnasts to warm up?
   ☐ 5 minutes  ☐ 15 minutes  ☐ 30 minutes

5. Which is the least likely injury to happen to a gymnast?
   ☐ broken leg  ☐ broken back  ☐ broken head

Name: _____

# Fact Or Opinion?

**Directions:** Read the numbered sentences and put an x in the corresponding numbered boxes to tell whether each sentence gives a fact or an opinion.

1. Gymnastics is probably the world's most exciting sport.

2. It's not fast-paced like basketball or hard-hitting like football.

3. Instead, it's a study in grace, strength and movement.

4. Floor exercises in gymnastics include such moves as swan dive to a forward roll, back handspring, forward handspring, the round off, and the backwards roll to a handstand with a twist.

5. These sound very complicated to me!

6. Moves used on the hanging rings include the basic hand swing, the forward hang turn, the forward swing uprise, and something called "the planche."

7. Whew! I'll bet the planche is really hard!

8. On the horizontal bar, gymnasts learn to do something called "the kip" and "the Hecht dismount."

9. My guess is the Hecht dismount is done when the gymnast gets off the bar.

10. If you're a scaredy-cat, that is probably your favorite move!

1. ☐ Fact ☐ Opinion
2. ☐ Fact ☐ Opinion
3. ☐ Fact ☐ Opinion
4. ☐ Fact ☐ Opinion
5. ☐ Fact ☐ Opinion
6. ☐ Fact ☐ Opinion
7. ☐ Fact ☐ Opinion
8. ☐ Fact ☐ Opinion
9. ☐ Fact ☐ Opinion
10. ☐ Fact ☐ Opinion

# Ring Stunts For Gymnasts

Gymnasts who excell at ring stunts must have very strong arms and shoulders. However, gymnastics coaches warn against weight lifting as a way of preparing for using the rings.

Why? Because ring stunts require a delicate combination of balance, coordination and strength. Muscular strength alone is not enough. Coaches say those who first build their muscles weight lifting tend to rely too much on strength and not enough on balance. As a result, their ring performances are not very graceful.

When doing ring stunts gymnasts must support their entire weight with their arms. If you think this is easy, try doing 10 chin-ups in a row on monkey bars. After number three—if you get that far—you will become a respectful admirer of ring stunts.

An especially difficult ring stunt is called the "wheel." While hanging from the rings, the gymnast turns his body in a full 360 degree circle—a slow "flip." Another very hard stunt is the "hang swing out." In this stunt, the gymnast gets in a handstand position on the rings, then swings down and out by bending and stretching his hips.

At the end of a ring routine, which includes several stunts, a gymnast often gets off the rings via a "somersault dismount." As he hits the peak of the upward movements of a forward swing, he does a somersault in the air before landing with both feet on the floor. The somersault dismount provides a dramatic conclusion to a gymnast's amazingly graceful show of strength and coordination.

**Directions:** Answer the questions about ring stunts.

1. Why do coaches warn against weight training for ring stunts?

_____

2. Which ring stunt requires a gymnast to turn in a 360 degree circle?

_____

3. Which is not a ring stunt?

☐ hang swing out   ☐ wheel   ☐ shoulder swing out

4. In the hang swing out, the gymnast first

☐ gets in a handstand position   ☐ gets in a wheel position

Name: _____

# Comparing Gymnastics Exercises

**Directions:** Read each paragraph, then answer the questions about making comparisons between ring stunts and floor exercises.

1. Ring stunts and floor exercises in gymnastics require different kinds of skills. The most obvious difference between the two is that the feet touch the floor in floor exercises.

What do the feet touch in ring stunts? _____

2. Both floor exercises and ring stunts require graceful movement and the ability to move smoothly from one stunt to another. Ring stunts require great strength in the arms and shoulders. Floor exercises require the gymnast to be sure-footed.

Do floor exercises require great arm and shoulder strength?

_____

3. Do ring stunts (prior to dismounting) require the gymnast to be

sure-footed? _____

4. Because they tend to have stronger upper bodies, men do better in ring exercises than women. However, many spectators insist that women are more exciting performers of floor exercises.

Compared to men, what do women excell at in gymnastics? _____

5. Because of their smaller size, Japanese men frequently outperform American men on ring stunts. Perhaps because they tend to have longer legs to swing around, American men find mastering ring stunts more of a challenge. This comparison does not hold true for floor exercises.

What factor seems to have no bearing on excelling at floor exercises?

_____

# Review

When gymnastics became popular at the beginning of this century, ring stunts requiring great strength were the most admired routines. Half a century later after World War II, ring routines grew to include swinging stunts as well. Today, performance on rings is divided into two categories.

The first category includes stunts that emphasize strength, such as holding the legs out straight while pushing the body up with the arms. In the second category are swinging stunts which display quick and graceful movement. Russians were the first gymnasts to perform a swinging stunt on rings. Their performance of "the wheel"—a full body flip—at the 1952 Olympics met with tremendous applause.

As with floor exercises, side horse, long horse, parallel bars and the horizontal bar, mastery of the rings requires a lot of practice. The final goal of all gymnastics routines is to combine a variety of moves and stunts into a performance that shows strength, flexibility and creativity.

**Directions:** Answer the questions about gymnastics.

1. Compare ring stunts at the turn of the century to gymnastics after World War II.

_____

2. Compared to the Russians, what did the other gymnasts at the 1952 Olympics lack?

_____

3. What stunts are in the second category of ring stunts? _____

4. Name six types of stunts.

1.)_____ 2.) _____ 3.) _____

4.)_____ 5.) _____ 6.) _____

Fact or opinion?

5. Russians are the best gymnasts in the world.    1. ☐ Fact ☐ Opinion

6. The Russians were the first to perform swinging stunts.    2. ☐ Fact ☐ Opinion

Name: _____

# The Ant And The Cricket

A silly young cricket who decided to sing—
Through the warm sunny months of summer and spring
Began to complain when he found that at home
His **cupboards** were empty and winter had come.

At last by starvation the cricket made bold
To hop through the wintertime snow and the cold
Away he set off to a **miserly** ant
To see if to keep him alive he would **grant**:
Shelter from rain, a mouthful of grain.
"I wish only to borrow—I'll repay it tomorrow—
If not, I must die of starvation and sorrow!"

Said the ant to the cricket, "It's true I'm your friend,
But we ants never borrow, we ants never lend;
We ants store up crumbs so when winter arrives
We have just enough food to keep ants alive."

**Directions:** Answer the questions about the poem.

1. Use context clues to choose the correct definition of "cupboards."

    ☐ where books are stored   ☐ where food is stored   ☐ where shoes are stored

2. Use context clues to choose the correct definition of "miserly."

    ☐ selfish/stingy   ☐ generous/kind   ☐ mean/ugly

3. Use context clue to choose the correct definition of "grant."

    ☐ to take away   ☐ to belch   ☐ to give

# Limericks

### Old Man From Peru

There was an old man from Peru
Who dreamed he was eating his shoe.
In the midst of the night
He awoke in a fright
And—good grief!—it was perfectly true.

### Old Man from Darjeeling

There was an old man from Darjeeling,
Who boarded a bus bound for Ealing.
He saw on the door:
"Please don't spit on the floor."
So he stood up and spat on the ceiling.

**Directions:** Answer the questions about these silly limericks.

1. In "Old Man From Peru," what was perfectly true?

_____

2. How did the old man from Peru feel when he awoke?

_____

3. In "Old Man From Darjeeling," what is Ealing?

_____

4. What did the old man from Darjeeling see on the door?

_____

5. Did the old man from Darjeeling break any rules?

_____

Name: _____

# Tree Toad

A tree toad loved a she-toad
Who lived up in a tree.
He was a two-toed tree toad
But a three-toed toad was she.
The two-toed tree toad tried to win
The three-toed she-toad's heart,
For the two-toed tree toad loved her—
She was lovely, kind and smart.
But the two-toed tree toad loved in vain,
He couldn't coax her down
She stayed alone up in the tree
While he cried on the ground.

**Directions:** Answer the questions about the poem.

1. How many toes did the female toad have?

_____

2. How many toes did the male toad have?

_____

3. Tell 3 reasons the male toad loved the she-toad?

_____

4. Why was the male toad's love in vain?

_____

5. What did he do in the end?

_____

# Three Silly Poems

**Poem #1**

I eat my peas with honey,
I've done it all my life.
It makes the peas taste funny—
But it keeps them on my knife!

**Poem #2**

At a restaurant that was quite new
A man found a mouse in his stew
Said the waiter, "Don't shout
Or wave it about,
Or the rest will be wanting one, too!"

**Poem #3**

If all the world were paper
And all the seas were ink,
And all the trees were bread and cheese,
What would the people think?

**Directions:** Answer the questions about the silly poems.

1. In poem #1, what's the purpose of the honey?

_____

2. What's the disadvantage to using honey?

_____

3. Why did the waiter tell the diner not to shout about the mouse he found?

_____

4. What were the world, the seas and the trees made of in poem #3?

_____

# I Saw A Ship A-Sailing

I saw a ship a-sailing,
A-sailing on the sea.
And, oh! it was all loaded
With tasty things for me.

There was candy in the cabin
And apples in the **hold**;
The sails were made of silk
The **masts** were made of gold.

The four-and-twenty sailors
That stood between the decks,
Were four-and-twenty white mice
With chains around their necks.

The captain was a duck,
With a **packet** on his back.
And when the ship began to move,
The captain said, "Quack! Quack!"

**Directions:** Answer the questions about the poem.

1. Use context clues to choose the correct definition of "hold."

☐ a place inside a ship    ☐ to squeeze or hug    ☐ a tear or rip

2. Use context clues to choose the correct definition of "masts."

☐ scarves covering the face    ☐ beams holding up a ship's sails

3. Use context clues to choose the correct definition of "packet."

☐ neck chain  ☐ backpack  ☐ two sails

# Old Gaelic Lullaby

Hush! The waves are rolling in,
White with foam, white with foam,
Father works amid the din.
But baby sleeps at home.

Hush! The winds roar hoarse and deep—
On they come, on they come!
Brother seek the wandering sheep,
But baby sleeps at home.

Hush! The rain sweeps over the fields
Where cattle roam, where cattle roam.
Sister goes to seek the cows
But baby sleeps at home.

**Directions:** Answer the questions about the Gaelic lullaby. (A Gaelic lullaby is an ancient Irish or Scottish song some parents sing as they rock their babies to sleep.)

1. What is father doing while baby sleeps?

_____

2. What is brother doing?

_____

3. What is sister doing?

_____

4. Is it quiet or noisy while father works?

☐ quiet    ☐ noisy

5. Which is **not** mentioned in the poem?

☐ wind    ☐ sunshine    ☐ waves    ☐ rain

Name: _____

# The Lark And The Wren

"Goodnight, Sir Wren!" said the little lark.
"The daylight fades; it will soon be dark.
I've bathed my wings in the sun's last ray,
I've sung my **hymn** to the parting day.
So now I fly to my quiet glen
In **yonder** meadow—Goodnight Wren!"

"Goodnight poor Lark," said the **haughty** wren
With a flick of his wing toward his happy friend.
"I also go to my rest **profound**
But not to sleep on the cold, damp ground.
The fittest place for a bird like me
Is the topmost **bough** of a tall pine tree."

**Directions:** Answer the questions about the poem.

1. Use context clues to choose the correct definition of "hymn."

☐ whisper    ☐ song    ☐ opposite of "her"

2. Use context clues to choose the correct definition of "yonder."

☐ nearby    ☐ mountaintop    ☐ seaside

3. Use context clues to choose the correct definition of "haughty."

☐ happy    ☐ friendly    ☐ stuck-up

4. Use context clues to choose the correct definition of "profound."

☐ restless    ☐ deep    ☐ uncomfortable

5. Use context clues to choose the correct definition of "bough."

☐ to bend over    ☐ tree roots    ☐ tree branch

Name: _____

# Review

### The Child And The Elves

The woods are full of elves tonight
The trees are all alive.
The river overflows with them
See how they swim and dive!
What funny little fellows
With pointed little ears
They dance and leap and **prance** and peep,
And yell out **elfin** cheers.

I'd like to tame just one of them
And keep him for myself.
I'd play with him the whole day long,
My funny little elf!
I'd teach my little elf to say "Yes sir,"
"thank you" and "please"
He'd even say "God bless you, dear!"
When anybody sneezed!

**Directions:** Answer the questions about the poem.

1. Use context clues to choose the correct definition of "prance."

   ☐ move in a slow way   ☐ move in a lively way

2. Use context clues to choose the correct definition of "elfin."

   ☐ elf-like   ☐ human-like   ☐ animal-like

3. What are the elves doing in the river? _____


4. What kind of ears do the elves have? _____


5. How many things would the boy teach the elf to say? _____

# The Gettysburg Address

*On November 19, 1863, President Abraham Lincoln gave a short speech to dedicate a cemetery of Civil War soldiers in Gettysburg, Pennsylvania where a famous battle was fought. He wrote five drafts of the Gettysburg Address, one of the most stirring speeches of all time. The war ended in 1865.*

Four score and seven years ago our fathers brought forth on this continent, a new nation, conceived in liberty, and dedicated to the proposition that all men are created equal.

Now we are engaged in a great civil war, testing whether that nation, or any nation so conceived and so dedicated, can long endure. We are met on a great battlefield of that war. We have come to dedicate a portion of that field as a final resting place for those who here gave their lives that this nation might live. It is altogether fitting and proper that we should do this.

But, in a larger sense, we cannot dedicate - we cannot consecrate - we cannot hallow - this ground. The brave men, living and dead, who struggled here have consecrated it far above our poor power to add or detract. The world will little note nor long remember what we say here, but it can never forget what they did here. It is for us the living, rather, to be dedicated to the unfinished work which they who fought here have thus far so nobly advanced. It is rather for us to be here dedicated to the great task remaining before us - that from these honored dead we take increased devotion to that cause for which they gave their last full measure of devotion - that we here highly resolve that these dead shall not have died in vain - that this nation, under God, shall have a new birth of freedom - and that government of the people, by the people, for the people shall not perish from this earth.

**Directions:** Answer the questions about the Gettysburg Address.

1. The main idea is

This speech will be long remembered as a tribute to the dead who died fighting in the Civil War.

This speech is to honor the dead soldiers who gave their lives so that the nation could have freedom for all citizens.

2. What battle was fought on the ground where the cemetery stood?

_____

# The Emancipation Proclamation

On September 22, 1862—a year before delivering the Gettysburg Adrress President Lincoln delivered The Emancipation Proclamation, which stated that all slaves in Confederate states should be set free.  Since the Confederate states had already withdrawn from the Union, they of course ignored the Proclamation.  The Proclamation did strengthen the north's war effort. About 200,000 black men—mostly former slaves—enlisted in the Union Army.  Two years later the 13th Amendment to the Constitution ended slavery in all parts of the United States.

I, Abraham Lincoln, do order and declare that all persons held as slaves within said designated States and parts of States are, and henceforward shall be, free; and that the Executive Government of the United States, including military and naval authorities thereof, shall recognize and maintain the freedom of said persons.

And I hereby enjoin upon the people so declared to be free to abstain from all violence, unless in necessary self-defense; and I recommend to them that, in all cases where allowed, they labor faithfully for reasonable wages.

And I further declare and make known that such persons of suitable condition will be received into the armed forces of the United States to garrison forts, positions, stations, and other places, and to man vessels of all sorts in said service.

*(This is not the full text of the Emancipation Proclamation.)*

**Directions:** Answer the questions about the Emancipation Proclamation.

1. How did the Emancipation Proclamation strengthen the north's war effort?

_____

2. Which came first, the Emancipation Proclamation or the Gettysburg Address?

_____

3. Which amendment to the constitution grew out of the Emancipation Proclamation?

_____

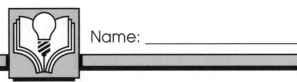

Name: _____

# Puzzling Out The Proclamation

**Directions:** Use the facts you learned about the Emancipation Proclamation to work the puzzle.

## Across

4. As a result of the Emancipation Proclamation came the 13th _____.
5. People who did not believe in slavery belonged to this army.
6. This part of the country slaves escaped to.

## Down

1. This President read the Emancipation Proclamation.
2. The Proclamation urged slaves to join the Union _____.
3. The part of the country the slaves left.

Name: _____

# Lincoln And The Southern States

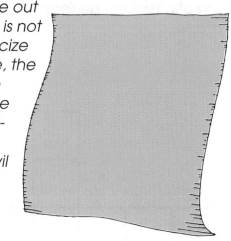

*Many people think that Abraham Lincoln had publicly come out against slavery from the beginning of his term as president. This is not the case. Whatever his private feelings, publicly he did not criticize slavery. Fearful that the southern states would secede, or leave, the union, he pledged to respect the southern states' rights to own slaves. He also pledged that the government would respect the southern states' runaway slave laws. These laws required all citizens to return runaway slaves to their masters.*

*Clearly, Lincoln did not want the country torn apart by a civil war. In the following statement, written in 1861 shortly after he became president, he makes it clear that the federal government will do its best to avoid conflict with the southern states.*

I hold that, in contemplation of the univeral law and of the Constitution, the Union of these states is perpetual. . . No state, upon its own mere motion, can lawfully get out of the Union. . . . I shall take care, as the Constitution itself expressly enjoins upon me, that the laws of the Union be faithfully executed in all the states. . . . The power confided to me will be used to hold, occupy, and possess the property and places belonging to the government, and to collect the duties and imposts. . . .

In your hands, my dissatisfied fellow-countrymen, and not in mine, is the momentous issue of civil war. The government will not assail you. You can have no conflict without yourselves being the aggressors. You have no oath registered in heaven to destroy the government, while I shall have the most solemn one to "preserve protect and defend" it.

**Directions:** Answer the questions about Lincoln and the southern states.

1. Use a dictionary to find the definition of "assail." _____

2. Use a dictionary to find the definition of "enjoin." _____

3. Use a dictionary to find the definition of "contemplation." _____

4. Lincoln is telling the southern states that the government

☐ does want a war    ☐ doesn't want a war    ☐ will stop a war

5. As president, Lincoln pledged to "preserve, protect and defend"

☐ slavery    ☐ the northern states    ☐ the union

Name: _____

# ...t Or Opinion?

...nces and put an x in the corresponding numbered
...gives a fact or an opinion.

2. I believe Lincoln thought the northern
states were the best because they
did not have slaves.

3. I think Lincoln did the right thing,
don't you?

4. The issues that sparked the Civil War
were complicated and difficult ones.

5. It would take an historian to really
understand them!

6. The "dissatisfied fellow-countrymen"
Lincoln refers to in his statement live
in the southern states.

7. As president, Lincoln took an oath to
"preserve, protect and defend" the
union, which included all the states.

8. Lincoln did his personal best to hold
the country together but it didn't do
one bit of good.

9. The Confederate States of America
had already been organized in February of 1861, a month before Lincoln
was sworn in as president.

10. Poor Abraham Lincoln—what a
crummy start to his presidency!

1. ☐ Fact ☐ Opinion

2. ☐ Fact ☐ Opinion

3. ☐ Fact ☐ Opinion

4. ☐ Fact ☐ Opinion

5. ☐ Fact ☐ Opinion

6. ☐ Fact ☐ Opinion

7. ☐ Fact ☐ Opinion

8. ☐ Fact ☐ Opinion

9. ☐ Fact ☐ Opinion

10. ☐ Fact ☐ Opinion

# Away Down South In Dixie

Although many southerners disapproved of slavery, the pressure to go along with the majority who supported slavery was very strong.  Many of those who thought slavery was wrong did not talk about their opinions. It was dangerous to do so!

The main reason the southern states seceded (withdrew) from the union in 1861 was because they wanted to protect their right to own slaves. They also wanted to increase the number of slaves so they could increase production of cotton and other crops that slaves tended.  Many Civil War monuments in the south are dedicated to a war that was described as "just and holy."

"Dixie," a song written in 1859 that is still popular in the south, sums up the attitude of many southerners. As the song lyrics show, southerners' loyalties lay not with the union representing all the states, but with the south and the southern way of life.

**Dixie**
*I wish I was in Dixie, Hoo-ray! Hoo-ray!*
*In Dixie land I'll take my stand*
*To live and die in Dixie.*
*Away, away, away down south in Dixie!*
*Away, away, away down south in Dixie!*

(*This is not the full text of the song.*)

1. Why did southerners who disapproved of slavery keep their opinions to themselves?

_____

2.  Why did southerners want more slaves?

_____

3. What are the words on some southern Civil War monuments?

_____

4. What "stand" is referred to in *Dixie*?

    ☐ stand for slavery   ☐ stand against slavery   ☐ stand for cotton

5. "Secede" means to

    ☐ quit    ☐ fight  ☐ withdraw

Name: _____

# Fact Or Opinion?

**Directions:** Read the numbered sentences and put an x in the corresponding numbered boxes to tell whether each sentence gives a fact or an opinion.

1. *Dixie* is a beautiful song!

2. It was written in 1859 by a man named Daniel Emmett, who died in 1904.

3. The song became a ralllying cry for southerners because it showed where their loyalties were.

4. I think their loyalty to slavery was absolutely wrong!

5. These four states where people owned slaves did not secede from the Union: Delaware, Maryland, Kentucky and Missouri.

6. The people in these states certainly made the right moral choice.

7. The ownership of one human being by another is absolutely and totally wrong under any circumstances.

8. In the states that did not secede from the union, some people fought for the Union and others fought for the Confederacy of Southern States.

9. Sometimes brothers fought against brothers on opposite sides of the war.

10. What a horrible situation to be in!

1. ☐ Fact ☐ Opinion

2. ☐ Fact ☐ Opinion

3. ☐ Fact ☐ Opinion

4. ☐ Fact ☐ Opinion

5. ☐ Fact ☐ Opinion

6. ☐ Fact ☐ Opinion

7. ☐ Fact ☐ Opinion

8. ☐ Fact ☐ Opinion

9. ☐ Fact ☐ Opinion

10. ☐ Fact ☐ Opinion

# Review

Although they were outnumbered, most southerners were convinced they could win the Civil War. The white population of the southern states was 5.5 million. The population was 18.9 million in the 19 states that stayed with the Union. Despite these odds, southerners felt history was on their side.

After all, the Colonists had been the underdogs against the British and had won the war for independence. Europeans also felt that Lincoln could not force the South to re-join the Union. The United Netherlands had successfully seceded from Spain. Greece had seceded from Turkey. Europeans were laying odds that two countries would take the place of what had once been the United States.

**Directions:** Answer the questions and work the puzzle.

1. What was the difference in population between the Union and Confederate states?

_____

2. The main idea is

   Although they were outnumbered, many people here and abroad felt the South would win the Civil War.

   Because they were outnumbered, the South knew winning the Civil War was a very long shot.

**Across**
4. They won the war of independence against England.
5. Did Europeans believe the South would win the war?
6. _____teen states belonged to the Union.

**Down**
1. Slaveowners lived in this area of the country.
2. The president during the Civil War.
3. To withdraw from the Union.

24

Name: _____

# Fun With Photography

The word photography means "writing with light." "Photo" is from the Greek word **photos** which means light. "Graphy" is from the Greek word **graphic** which means writing. Cameras don't literally write pictures of course. Instead, they imprint an image onto a piece of film.

Even the most sophisticated camera is basically a box with a piece of light sensitive film inside a box. The box has a hole at the opposite end from the film. The light enters the box from the hole—the camera's lens—and shines on the surface of the film to create a picture. The picture that's created on the film is the image the camera's lens is pointed toward.

A **lens** is a circle of glass that is thinner at the edges and thicker in the center. The outer edges of the lens collect the light rays and draw them together at the center of the lens.

The **shutter** helps control the amount of light that enters the lens. Too much light will make the picture too light. Too little light will result in a dark picture. Electronic flash—either built into the camera or attached to the top of it—provides light when needed.

Cameras with automatic electronic flashes will provide the additional light automatically. Electronic flashes—or "flashes" as they are often called—require batteries. If your automatic flash or flash attachment quits working, a dead battery is probably the cause.

**Directions:** Answer the questions about photography.

1. From what language is the word "photography" derived?

_____

2. Where is the camera lens thickest?

_____

3. What do the outer edges of the lens do?

_____

4. When is a flash needed?

_____

5. What does the shutter do?

_____

# Photography Terms

Like other good professionals, photographers make their craft look easy. Their skill—like that of the graceful ice skater—comes from years of practice. Where skaters develop a sense of balance, photographers develop an "eye" for pictures. They can make important technical decisions about a photographing, or "shooting," a particular scene in the twinkling of an eye.

It's interesting to know some of the technical language that professional photographers use. "Angle of view" refers to the angle from which a photograph is taken. "Depth of field" is the distance between the nearest point and the farthest point in a photo that is in focus.

"Filling the frame" refers to the amount of space the object being photographed takes up in the picture. A close-up picture of a dog, flower or person would fill the frame. A far-away picture would not.

"ASA" refers to the speed of different types of films. "Speed" means the film's sensitivity to light. The letters ASA stand for the American Standards Association. Film manufacturers give their films ratings of 200ASA, 400ASA, etc. to indicate film speed. The higher the number on the film, the higher its sensitivity to light and the faster its speed. The faster its speed, the better it will be at clearly capturing sports images and other action shots.

**Directions:** Answer the questions about photography terms.

1. Name another term for photographing. _____

2. This is the distance between the nearest point and the farthest point of a photo that's in

focus. _____

3. This refers to the speed of different types of film. _____

4. A close-up picture of someone's face would

☐ provide depth of field   ☐ create an ASA   ☐ fill the frame

5. To photograph a swimming child, which film speed is better?

☐ 200ASA   ☐ 400ASA

Name: _____

# Photography Puzzler

**Directions:** Use the facts you have learned about photography to work the puzzle.

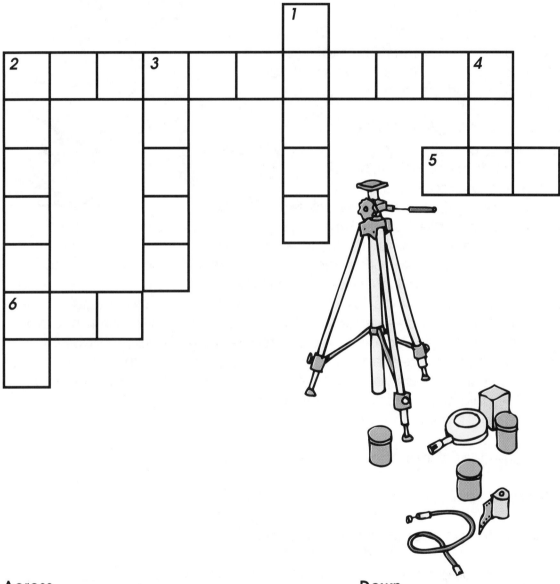

**Across**

2. A film's speed indicates its _____ to light.
6. Good photographers develop an ____ for pictures.
5. Stands for the American Standards Association.

**Down**

1. This is what the Greek word "photos" means.
2. This helps control the amount of light entering the lens.
3. This term refers to the film's sensitivity to light.
4. Would a close-up picture of a cat fill the frame?

Name: _____

# Photographing Animals

Animals are a favorite subject of many young photographers. Cats, dogs, hamsters and other pets top the list, followed by zoo animals and the occasional lizard.

Because it's hard to get them to sit still and "perform on command," many professional photographers joke that—given a choice—they will refuse to photograph pets or small children. There **are** ways around the problem of short attention spans, however.

One way to get an appealing portrait of a cat or dog is to hold a biscuit or treat above the camera. The animal's longing look toward the food will be captured by the camera as a soulful gaze. Because it's above the camera—out of the camera's range—the treat won't appear in the picture. When you show the picture to your friends afterwards they will be impressed by your pet's loving expression.

If you are using fast film, you can take some good, quick shots of pets by simply snapping a picture right after calling their names. You'll get a different expression from your pet using this technique. Depending on your pet's disposition, the picture will capture an inquisitive expression or possibly a look of annoyance—especially if you've awakened Rover from a nap!

To photograph zoo animals, put the camera as close to the animal's cage as possible so you can shoot between the bars or wire mesh. Wild animals don't respond the same way as pets—after all, they don't know you!—so you will have to be more patient to capture a good shot. If it's legal to feed the animals, you can get their attention by having a friend toss them treats as you concentrate on shooting some good pictures.

**Directions:** Answer the questions about photographing animals.

1. Why do some professionals dislike photographing animals? _____

2. What speed film should you use to photograph quick-moving pets? _____

3. To capture a pet's loving expression, hold this out of camera range. _____

4. For a good picture of zoo animals

☐ get close to the cage      ☐ stand back from the cage

5. To get a zoo animal's attention, who should toss them treats?

☐ the photographer      ☐ a friend      ☐ a zoo keeper

Name: _____

# Generalization

A generalization is a statement of principle that applies in many different situations.

**Directions:** Read each passage and circle the valid generalization.

1. Most people can quickly be taught to use a simple camera. However, it takes time, talent and a good eye to learn to take professional quality photographs. Patience is another quality that good photographers must possess. Those who photograph nature often will wait hours to get just the right light or shadow in their pictures.

a. There's no one who can't learn to use a camera.
b. Any patient person can become a good photographer.
c. Good photographers have a good eye for pictures.

2. Photographers such as Diane Arbus, who photograph strange or odd people, also must wait for just the right picture. Many "people photographers" stake out a busy city sidewalk and study the faces of crowds. Then they must leap up quickly and ask to take a picture—or sneakily take one without being observed. Either way, it's not an easy task!

a. Staking out a busy city sidewalk is a boring task.
b. "People photographers" must be patient people and good observers.
c. Sneak photography is not a nice thing to do to strangers.

3. Whether the subject is nature or humans, many photographers insist that dawn is the best time to take pictures. The light is clear at this early hour, and mist may still be in the air. The mist gives these early morning photos a haunting, "other world" quality that is very appealing.

a. Morning mist gives an unusual quality to most outdoor photographs.
b. Photographers all agree that dawn is the best time to take pictures.
c. Misty light is always important in taking all pictures.

Name: _____

# Camera Care

Camera dealers say many amateur photographers should take better care of their cameras. Too often, people carelessly leave expensive cameras laying out where young children or pets can get hold of them. They fail to keep put cameras back into the carrying cases that protect them. They take them to the beach and leave them laying in the sand. Another way people ruin their cameras is by leaving them for days inside a hot car.

Because they must carry so many attachments, professional photographers keep their cameras inside a large, soft shoulder bag. The bag provides extra protection for the camera, which is also protected by its camera case.

Inside the bag are compartments for film, extra lenses and other attachments. Other equipment inside a professional photographer's bag may include the following: lens hood, cable release, filters and holder, cleaning cloth and screw driver. A photographer's bag is filled with all sorts of interesting things!

Flashlights, pens, tape and sometimes a sandwich for lunch may fill out the odd assortment of objects. In addition, many photographers carry a tripod to set the camera on for still pictures. Can you see why photographers usually develop strong arm and shoulder muscles?

**Directions:** Answer the questions about caring for and storing cameras.

1. Name four ways people abuse their cameras.

1._____    2._____

3._____    4._____

2. What do professional photographers carry their equipment in?

_____

3. Which of the following is **not** in a photographer's bag?

☐ lens hood      ☐ tripod    ☐ lens filters

4. Photographers often develop which set of muscles?

☐ legs and feet    ☐ arms and shoulders    ☐ head and neck

# ANSWER KEY

*This Answer Key has been designed so that it may be easily removed if you so desire.*

## MASTER COMPREHENSION
## 6

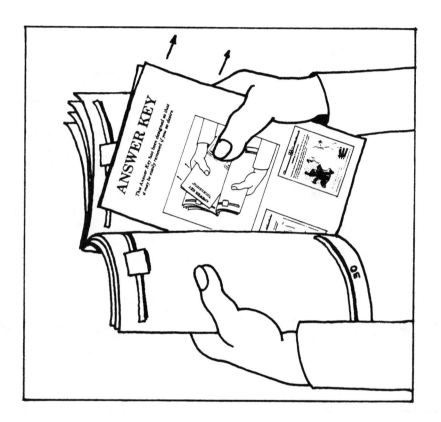

---

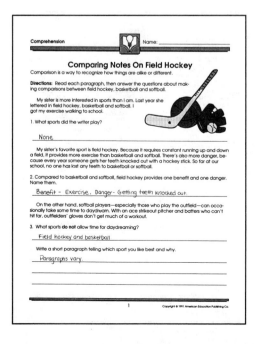

Comprehension                     Name: _____

### Comparing Notes On Field Hockey

Comparison is a way to recognize how things are alike or different.

**Directions:** Read each paragraph, then answer the questions about making comparisons between field hockey, basketball and softball.

My sister is more interested in sports than I am. Last year she lettered in field hockey, basketball and softball. I got my exercise walking to school.

1. What sports did the writer play?

   None

My sister's favorite sport is field hockey. Because it requires constant running up and down a field, it provides more exercise than basketball and softball. There's also more danger, because every year someone gets her teeth knocked out with a hockey stick. So far at our school, no one has lost any teeth to basketball or softball.

2. Compared to basketball and softball, field hockey provides one benefit and one danger. Name them.

   Benefit - Exercise.  Danger- Getting teeth knocked out.

On the other hand, softball players—especially those who play the outfield—can occasionally take some time to daydream. With an ace strikeout pitcher and batters who can't hit far, outfielders' gloves don't get much of a workout.

3. What sports do **not** allow time for daydreaming?

   Field hockey and basketball

Write a short paragraph telling which sport you like best and why.

   Paragraphs vary.
   _____
   _____
   _____

---

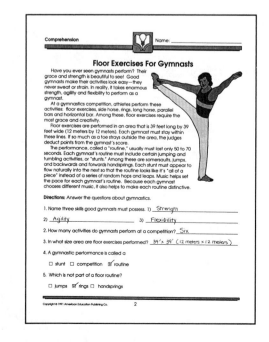

Comprehension                     Name: _____

### Floor Exercises For Gymnasts

Have you ever seen gymnasts perform? Their grace and strength is beautiful to see! Good gymnasts make their activities look easy—they never sweat or strain. In reality, it takes enormous strength, agility and flexibility to perform as a gymnast.

At a gymnastics competition, athletes perform these activities: floor exercises, side horse, rings, long horse, parallel bars and horizontal bar. Among these, floor exercises require the most grace and creativity.

Floor exercises are performed in an area that is 39 feet long by 39 feet wide (12 meters by 12 meters). Each gymnast must stay within these lines. If so much as a toe strays outside the area, the judges deduct points from the gymnast's score.

The performance, called a "routine," usually must last only 50 to 70 seconds. Each gymnast's routine must include certain jumping and tumbling activities, or "stunts." Among these are somersaults, jumps, and backwards and forwards handsprings. Each stunt must appear to flow naturally into the next so that the routine looks like it's "all of a piece" instead of a series of random hops and leaps. Music helps set the pace for each gymnast's routine. Because each gymnast chooses different music, it also helps to make each routine distinctive.

**Directions:** Answer the questions about gymnastics.

1. Name three skills good gymnasts must possess. 1) Strength

2) Agility                                3) Flexibility

2. How many activities do gymnasts perform at a competition? Six

3. In what size area are floor exercises performed? 39'x 39' (12 meters x 12 meters)

4. A gymnastic performance is called a

   ☐ stunt  ☐ competition  ☑ routine

5. Which is not part of a floor routine?

   ☐ jumps  ☑ rings  ☐ handsprings

## Fact Or Opinion?

A fact can be proved. An opinion, which cannot be proved, tells what someone believes.

**Directions:** Read the numbered sentences and put an x in the corresponding numbered boxes to tell whether each sentence gives a fact or an opinion.

1. Gymnasts are the most exciting athletes to watch!   1. ☐ Fact ☒ Opinion

2. Because their sport requires all-over body strength, gymnasts must have very strong arms and legs. Their stomach muscles and the muscles in their feet must also be in good condition.   2. ☒ Fact ☐ Opinion

3. To do handstands, gymnasts must support the weight of their upside-down bodies by holding their hands flat and their arms straight. Their legs must be pointed straight up.   3. ☒ Fact ☐ Opinion

4. With a little practice, I think anyone could learn to do a handstand.   4. ☐ Fact ☒ Opinion

5. A somersault is more difficult than a handstand.   5. ☐ Fact ☒ Opinion

6. It requires starting and stopping from a standing position after making a 360-degree turn in the air.   6. ☒ Fact ☐ Opinion

7. I'll bet not many people can do a good somersault!   7. ☐ Fact ☒ Opinion

8. Some of the different kinds of somersaults are backwards somersaults, sideways somersaults and something called a "bent body" somersault.   8. ☒ Fact ☐ Opinion

9. I've never seen a bent body somersault, but I think it must require a lot of bending.   9. ☐ Fact ☒ Opinion

10. I don't think I would be any good at the bent body somersault.   10. ☐ Fact ☒ Opinion

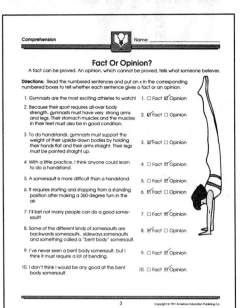

---

## Warming Up To Gymnastics

Because no bats, racquets or balls are used, some people mistakenly believe that gymnastics is not a dangerous sport. Although major injuries don't happen often, broken legs—as well as broken necks and backs—can occur. The reason they don't happen frequently is that gymnasts follow safety rules that help prevent accidents.

One thing gymnasts are careful to do every time they practice their sport is to first warm up their muscles. "Warm-ups" are exercises that gently stretch and loosen the muscles before subjecting them to tension and strain.

Warm-ups help the muscles gradually expand and stretch so they move efficiently during vigorous exercise. Without a warm-up of 15 to 30 minutes it's possible that unworked muscles will be dangerously pulled or strained. Because a muscle injury can interfere with—or stop—an athlete's performance, experienced gymnasts never skip or rush through their warm-ups.

Another thing gymnasts do to help prevent accidents is to use "spotters" when they practice. Spotters are people—usually other gymnasts—who stand beside gymnasts when they are practicing new movements. If gymnasts twist the wrong way or begin to fall, spotters will grab them to prevent injury. Spotters also often offer helpful advice and instant feedback on gymnasts' performances.

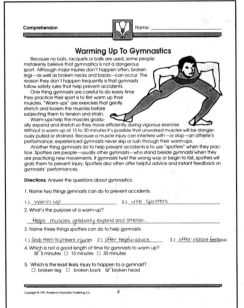

**Directions:** Answer the questions about gymnastics.

1. Name two things gymnasts can do to prevent accidents.

1.) _warm up_          2.) _use spotters_

2. What's the purpose of a warm-up?

_Helps muscles gradually expand and stretch._

3. Name three things spotters can do to help gymnasts.

1.) _Grab them to prevent injuries_ 2.) _offer helpful advice_ 3.) _offer instant feedback_

4. Which is not a good length of time for gymnasts to warm up?
   ☒ 5 minutes ☐ 15 minutes ☐ 30 minutes

5. Which is the least likely injury to happen to a gymnast?
   ☐ broken leg ☐ broken back ☒ broken head

---

## Fact Or Opinion?

**Directions:** Read the numbered sentences and put an x in the corresponding numbered boxes to tell whether each sentence gives a fact or an opinion.

1. Gymnastics is probably the world's most exciting sport.

2. It's not fast-paced like basketball or hard-hitting like football.

3. Instead, it's a study in grace, strength and movement.

4. Floor exercises include such moves as swan dive to a forward roll, back handspring, forward handspring, the round off, and the backwards roll to a handstand with a twist.

5. These sound very complicated to me!

6. Moves used on the hanging rings include the basic hand swing, the forward hang turn, the forward swing uprise, and something called "the planche."

7. Whew! I'll bet the planche is really hard!

8. On the horizontal bar, gymnasts learn to do something called "the kip" and "the Hecht dismount."

9. My guess is the Hecht dismount is done when the gymnast gets off the bar.

10. If you're a scaredy-cat, that is probably your favorite move!

1. ☐ Fact ☒ Opinion
2. ☒ Fact ☐ Opinion
3. ☒ Fact ☐ Opinion
4. ☒ Fact ☐ Opinion
5. ☐ Fact ☒ Opinion
6. ☒ Fact ☐ Opinion
7. ☐ Fact ☒ Opinion
8. ☒ Fact ☐ Opinion
9. ☐ Fact ☒ Opinion
10. ☐ Fact ☒ Opinion

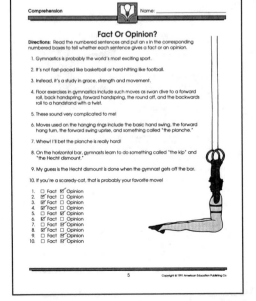

---

## Ring Stunts For Gymnasts

Gymnasts who excel at ring stunts must have very strong arms and shoulders. However, gymnastics coaches warn against weight lifting as a way of preparing for using the rings.

Why? Because ring stunts require a delicate combination of balance, coordination and strength. Muscular strength alone is not enough. Coaches say those who first build their muscles weight lifting tend to rely too much on strength and not enough on balance. As a result, their ring performances are not very graceful.

When doing ring stunts gymnasts must support their entire weight with their arms. If you think this is easy, try doing 10 chin-ups in a row on monkey bars. After number three—if you get that far—you will become a respectful admirer of ring stunts.

An especially difficult ring stunt is called the "wheel." While hanging from the rings, the gymnast turns his body in a full 360 degree circle—a slow "flip." Another very hard stunt is the "hang swing out." In this stunt, the gymnast gets in a handstand position on the rings, then swings down and out by bending and stretching his hips.

At the end of a ring routine, which includes several stunts, a gymnast often gets off the rings via a "somersault dismount." As he hits the peak of the upward movements of a forward swing, he does a somersault in the air before landing with both feet on the floor. The somersault dismount provides a dramatic conclusion to a gymnast's amazingly graceful show of strength and coordination.

**Directions:** Answer the questions about ring stunts.

1. Why do coaches warn against weight training for ring stunts?

_To prevent too much reliance on strength and not enough on balance._

2. Which ring stunt requires a gymnast to turn in a 360 degree circle?

_Wheel_

3. Which is not a ring stunt?

☐ hang swing out ☐ wheel ☒ shoulder swing out

4. In the hang swing out, the gymnast first

☒ gets in a handstand position ☐ gets in a wheel position

---

## Comparing Gymnastics Exercises

**Directions:** Read each paragraph, then answer the questions about making comparisons between ring stunts and floor exercises.

1. Ring stunts and floor exercises in gymnastics require different kinds of skills. The most obvious difference between the two is that the feet touch the floor in floor exercises.

What do the feet touch in ring stunts? _Nothing_

2. Both floor exercises and ring stunts require graceful movement and the ability to move smoothly from one stunt to another. Ring stunts require great strength in the arms and shoulders. Floor exercises require the gymnast to be sure-footed.

Do floor exercises require great arm and shoulder strength?

_No_

3. Do ring stunts (prior to dismounting) require the gymnast to be

sure-footed? _No_

4. Because they tend to have stronger upper bodies, men do better in ring exercises than women. However, many spectators insist that women are more exciting performers of floor exercises.

Compared to men, what do women excel at in gymnastics? _Floor exercises_

5. Because of their smaller size, Japanese men frequently outperform American men on ring stunts. Perhaps because they tend to have longer legs to swing around, American men find mastering ring stunts more of a challenge. This comparison does not hold true for floor exercises.

What factor seems to have no bearing at excelling at floor exercises?

_Small size_

---

## Review

When gymnastics became popular at the beginning of this century, ring stunts requiring great strength were the most admired routines. Half a century later after World War II, ring routines grew to include swinging stunts as well. Today, performance on rings is divided into two categories.

The first category are stunts that emphasize strength, such as holding the legs out straight while pushing the body up with the arms. In the second category are swinging stunts which display quick and graceful movement. Russians were the first gymnasts to perform a swinging stunt on rings. Their performance of "the wheel"—a full body flip—at the 1952 Olympics met with tremendous applause.

As with floor exercises, side horse, long horse, parallel bars and the horizontal bar, mastery of the rings requires a lot of practice. The final goal of all gymnastics routines is to combine a variety of moves and stunts into a performance that shows strength, flexibility and creativity.

**Directions:** Answer the questions about gymnastics.

1. Compare ring stunts at the turn of the century to gymnastics after World War II.

_There were not swinging stunts before W.W.II._

2. Compared to the Russians, what did the other gymnasts at the 1952 Olympics lack?

_The ability to do swinging stunts._

3. What stunts are in the second category of ring stunts? _Swinging stunts_

4. Name six types of stunts.

1.) _Ring_          2.) _floor exercises_          3.) _side horse_

4.) _long horse_          5.) _parallel bars_          6.) _horizontal bar_

Fact or opinion?

5. Russians are the best gymnasts in the world.   1. ☐ Fact ☒ Opinion

6. The Russians were the first to perform swinging stunts.   2. ☒ Fact ☐ Opinion

## The Ant And The Cricket

A silly young cricket who decided to sing—
Through the warm sunny months of summer and spring
Began to complain when he found that at home
His **cupboards** were empty and winter had come.

At last by starvation the cricket made bold
To hop through the wintertime snow and the cold
Away he set off to a **miserly** ant
To see if to keep him alive he would **grant**:
Shelter from rain, a mouthful of grain.
"I wish only to borrow—I'll repay it tomorrow—
If not, I must die of starvation and sorrow!"

Said the ant to the cricket, "It's true I'm your friend,
But we ants never borrow, we ants never lend;
We ants store up crumbs so when winter arrives
We have just enough food to keep ants alive."

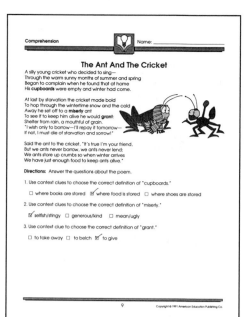

**Directions:** Answer the questions about the poem.

1. Use context clues to choose the correct definition of "cupboards."

☐ where books are stored  ☑ where food is stored  ☐ where shoes are stored

2. Use context clues to choose the correct definition of "miserly."

☑ selfish/stingy  ☐ generous/kind  ☐ mean/ugly

3. Use context clue to choose the correct definition of "grant."

☐ to take away  ☐ to belch  ☑ to give

---

## Three Silly Poems

**Poem #1**

I eat my peas with honey,
I've done it all my life.
It makes the peas taste funny—
But it keeps them on my knife!

**Poem #2**

At a restaurant that was quite new
A man found a mouse in his stew
Said the waiter, "Don't shout
Or wave it about,
Or the rest will be wanting one, too!"

**Poem #3**

If all the world were paper
And all the seas were ink,
And all the trees were bread and cheese,
What would the people think?

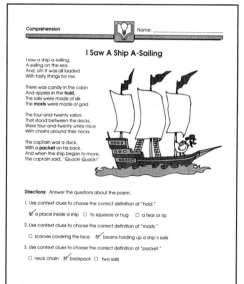

**Directions:** Answer the questions about the silly poems.

1. In poem #1, what's the purpose of the honey?

To stick the peas to the knife.

2. What's the disadvantage to using honey?

The peas taste funny.

3. Why did the waiter tell the diner not to shout about the mouse he found?

Because others would want one, too!

4. What were the world, the seas and the trees made of in poem #3?

Paper, ink, bread and cheese.

---

## Limericks

**Old Man From Peru**

There was an old man from Peru
Who dreamed he was eating his shoe.
In the midst of the night
He awoke in a fright
And—good grief!—it was perfectly true.

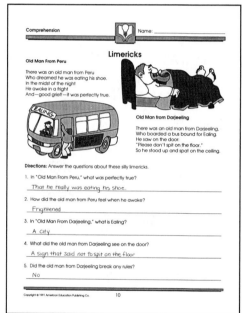

**Old Man from Darjeeling**

There was an old man from Darjeeling,
Who boarded a bus bound for Ealing.
He saw on the door:
"Please don't spit on the floor."
So he stood up and spat on the ceiling.

**Directions:** Answer the questions about these silly limericks.

1. In "Old Man From Peru," what was perfectly true?

That he really was eating his shoe.

2. How did the old man from Peru feel when he awoke?

Frightened

3. In "Old Man From Darjeeling," what is Ealing?

A city.

4. What did the old man from Darjeeling see on the door?

A sign that said not to spit on the floor

5. Did the old man from Darjeeling break any rules?

No

---

## I Saw A Ship A-Sailing

I saw a ship a-sailing,
A-sailing on the sea.
And, oh! it was all loaded
With tasty things for me.

There was candy in the cabin
And apples in the **hold**.
The sails were made of silk
The **masts** were made of gold.

The four-and-twenty sailors
That stood between the decks,
Were four-and-twenty white mice
With chains around their necks.

The captain was a duck,
With a **packet** on his back.
And when the ship began to move,
The captain said, "Quack! Quack!"

**Directions:** Answer the questions about the poem.

1. Use context clues to choose the correct definition of "hold."

☑ a place inside a ship  ☐ to squeeze or hug  ☐ a tear or rip

2. Use context clues to choose the correct definition of "masts."

☐ scarves covering the face  ☑ beams holding up a ship's sails

3. Use context clues to choose the correct definition of "packet."

☐ neck chain  ☑ backpack  ☐ two sails

---

## Tree Toad

A tree toad loved a she-toad
Who lived up in a tree.
He was a two-toed tree toad
But a three-toed tree toad was she.
The two-toed tree toad tried to win
The three-toed she-toad's heart,
For the two-toed tree toad loved her—
She was lovely, kind and smart.
But the two-toed tree toad loved in vain,
He couldn't coax her down
She stayed alone up in the tree
While he cried on the ground.

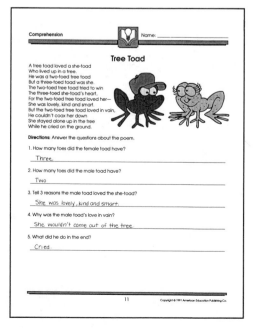

**Directions:** Answer the questions about the poem.

1. How many toes did the female toad have?

Three

2. How many toes did the male toad have?

Two

3. Tell 3 reasons the male toad loved the she-toad?

She was lovely, kind and smart.

4. Why was the male toad's love in vain?

She wouldn't come out of the tree.

5. What did he do in the end?

Cried.

---

## Old Gaelic Lullaby

Hush! The waves are rolling in,
White with foam, white with foam,
Father works amid the din,
But baby sleeps at home.

Hush! The winds roar hoarse and deep—
On they come, on they come!
Brother seek the wandering sheep,
But baby sleeps at home.

Hush! The rain sweeps over the fields
Where cattle roam, where cattle roam.
Sister goes to seek the cows
But baby sleeps at home.

**Directions:** Answer the questions about the Gaelic lullaby. (A Gaelic lullaby is an ancient Irish or Scottish song some parents sing as they rock their babies to sleep.)

1. What is father doing while baby sleeps?

Working

2. What is brother doing?

Looking for lost sheep.

3. What is sister doing?

Looking for the cows.

4. Is it quiet or noisy while father works?

☐ quiet  ☑ noisy

5. Which is **not** mentioned in the poem?

☐ wind  ☑ sunshine  ☐ waves  ☐ rain

Name: _____

## The Lark And The Wren

"Goodnight, Sir Wren!" said the little lark.
"The daylight fades; it will soon be dark.
I've bathed my wings in the sun's last ray,
I've sung my **hymn** to the parting day.
So now I fly to my quiet glen
In **yonder** meadow—Goodnight Wren!"

"Goodnight poor Lark," said the **haughty** wren
With a flick of his wing toward his happy friend.
"I also go to my rest **profound**
But not to sleep on the cold, damp ground.
The fittest place for a bird like me
Is the topmost **bough** of a tall pine tree."

**Directions:** Answer the questions about the poem.

1. Use context clues to choose the correct definition of "hymn."

☐ whisper   ☑ song   ☐ opposite of "her"

2. Use context clues to choose the correct definition of "yonder."

☑ nearby   ☐ mountaintop   ☐ seaside

3. Use context clues to choose the correct definition of "haughty."

☐ happy   ☐ friendly   ☑ stuck-up

4. Use context clues to choose the correct definition of "profound."

☐ restless   ☑ deep   ☐ uncomfortable

5. Use context clues to choose the correct definition of "bough."

☐ to bend over   ☐ tree roots   ☑ tree branch

---

## Review

**The Child And The Elves**

The woods are full of elves tonight
The trees are all alive.
The river overflows with them
See how they swim and dive!
What funny little fellows
With pointed little ears
They dance and leap and **prance** and peep,
And yell out **elfin** cheers.

I'd like to tame just one of them
And keep him for myself.
I'd play with him the whole day long,
My funny little elf!
I'd teach my little elf to say "Yes sir,"
"thank you" and "please"
He'd even say "God bless you, dear!"
When anybody sneezed!

**Directions:** Answer the questions about the poem.

1. Use context clues to choose the correct definition of "prance."

☐ move in a slow way   ☑ move in a lively way

2. Use context clues to choose the correct definition of "elfin."

☑ elf-like   ☐ human-like   ☐ animal-like

3. What are the elves doing in the river? _Swimming_

4. What kind of ears do the elves have? _Pointed_

5. How many things would the boy teach the elf to say? _Four_

---

## The Gettysburg Address

*On November 19, 1863, President Abraham Lincoln gave a short speech to dedicate a cemetery of Civil War soldiers in Gettysburg, Pennsylvania where a famous battle was fought. He wrote five drafts of the Gettysburg Address, one of the most stirring speeches of all time. The war ended in 1865.*

Four score and seven years ago our fathers brought forth on this continent, a new nation, conceived in liberty, and dedicated to the proposition that all men are created equal.

Now we are engaged in a great civil war, testing whether that nation, or any nation so conceived and so dedicated, can long endure. We are met on a great battlefield of that war. We have come to dedicate a portion of that field as a final resting place for those who here gave their lives that this nation might live. It is altogether fitting and proper that we should do this.

But, in a larger sense, we cannot dedicate - we cannot consecrate - we cannot hallow - this ground. The brave men, living and dead, who struggled here have consecrated it far above our poor power to add or detract. The world will little note nor long remember what we say here, but it can never forget what they did here. It is for us the living, rather, to be dedicated to the unfinished work which they who fought here have thus far so nobly advanced. It is rather for us to be here dedicated to the great task remaining before us - that from these honored dead we take increased devotion to that cause for which they gave their last full measure of devotion - that we here highly resolve that these dead shall not have died in vain - that this nation, under God, shall have a new birth of freedom - and that government of the people, by the people, for the people shall not perish from this earth.

**Directions:** Answer the questions about the Gettysburg Address.

1. The main idea is

☐ This speech will be long remembered as a tribute to the dead who died fighting in the Civil War.

☑ This speech is to honor the dead soldiers who gave their lives so that the nation could have freedom for all citizens.

2. What battle was fought on the ground where the cemetery stood?
_Gettysburg_

---

## The Emancipation Proclamation

*On September 22, 1862—a year before delivering the Gettysburg Address President Lincoln delivered The Emancipation Proclamation, which stated that all slaves in Confederate states should be set free. Since the Confederate states had already withdrawn from the Union, they of course ignored the Proclamation. The Proclamation did strengthen the north's war effort. About 200,000 black men—mostly former slaves—enlisted in the Union Army. Two years later the 13th Amendment to the Constitution ended slavery in all parts of the United States.*

I, Abraham Lincoln, do order and declare that all persons held as slaves within said designated States and parts of States are, and henceforward shall be, free; and that the Executive Government of the United States, including military and naval authorities thereof, shall recognize and maintain the freedom of said persons.

And I hereby enjoin upon the people so declared to be free to abstain from all violence, unless in necessary self-defense; and I recommend to them that, in all cases where allowed, they labor faithfully for reasonable wages.

And I further declare and make known that such persons of suitable condition will be received into the armed forces of the United States to garrison forts, positions, stations, and other places, and to man vessels of all sorts in said service.
*(This is not the full text of the Emancipation Proclamation.)*

**Directions:** Answer the questions about the Emancipation Proclamation.

1. How did the Emancipation Proclamation strengthen the north's war effort?

_By allowing black men to join the Union Army - 200,000 of them did_

2. Which came first, the Emancipation Proclamation or the Gettysburg Address?

_Emancipation Proclamation_

3. Which amendment to the constitution grew out of the Emancipation Proclamation?

_13th Amendment_

---

## Puzzling Out The Proclamation

**Directions:** Use the facts you learned about the Emancipation Proclamation to work the puzzle.

Crossword answers:
1 down: LINCOLN
2 down: ARMY
3 down: SOUTH
4 across: AMENDMENT
5 across: UNION
6 across: NORTH

**Across**

4. As a result of the Emancipation Proclamation came the 13th _____
5. People who did not believe in slavery belonged to this army.
6. This part of the country slaves escaped to.

**Down**

1. This President read the Emancipation Proclamation.
2. The Proclamation urged slaves to join the Union _____
3. The part of the country the slaves left.

---

## Lincoln And The Southern States

*Many people think that Abraham Lincoln had publicly come out against slavery from the beginning of his term as president. This is not the case. Whatever his private feelings, publicly he did not criticize slavery. Fearful that the southern states would secede, or leave, the union, he pledged to respect the southern states' rights to own slaves. He also pledged that the government would respect the southern states' runaway slave laws. These laws required all citizens to return runaway slaves to their masters.*

*Clearly, Lincoln did not want the country torn apart by a civil war. In the following statement, written in 1861 shortly after he became president, he makes it clear that the federal government will do its best to avoid conflict with the southern states.*

I hold that, in contemplation of the univeral law and of the Constitution, the Union of these states is perpetual. . . No state, upon its own mere motion, can lawfully get out of the Union. . . . I shall take care, as the Constitution itself expressly enjoins upon me, that the laws of the Union be faithfully executed in all the states. . . . The power confided to me will be used to hold, occupy, and possess the property and places belonging to the government, and to collect the duties and imposts. . . .

In your hands, my dissatisfied fellow-countrymen, and not in mine, is the momentous issue of civil war. The government will not assail you. You can have no conflict without yourselves being the aggressors. You have no oath registered in heaven to destroy the government, while I shall have the most solemn one to "preserve protect and defend" it.

**Directions:** Answer the questions about Lincoln and the southern states.

1. Use a dictionary to find the definition of "assail." _Physically attack_

2. Use a dictionary to find the definition of "enjoin." _To order_

3. Use a dictionary to find the definition of "contemplation." _The study of_

4. Lincoln is telling the southern states that the government

☐ does want a war   ☑ doesn't want a war   ☐ will stop a war

5. As president, Lincoln pledged to "preserve, protect and defend"

☐ slavery   ☐ the northern states   ☑ the union

## Fact Or Opinion?

**Directions:** Read the numbered sentences and put an x in the corresponding numbered boxes to tell whether each sentence gives a fact or an opinion.

1. Lincoln warned the southern states that they could not legally leave the union.
   1. ☒ Fact ☐ Opinion

2. I believe Lincoln thought the northern states were the best because they did not have slaves.
   2. ☐ Fact ☒ Opinion

3. I think Lincoln did the right thing, don't you?
   3. ☐ Fact ☒ Opinion

4. The issues that sparked the Civil War were complicated and difficult ones.
   4. ☒ Fact ☐ Opinion

5. It would take an historian to really understand them!
   5. ☐ Fact ☒ Opinion

6. The "dissatisfied fellow-countrymen" Lincoln refers to in his statement live in the southern states.
   6. ☒ Fact ☐ Opinion

7. As president, Lincoln took an oath to "preserve, protect and defend" the union, which included all the states.
   7. ☒ Fact ☐ Opinion

8. Lincoln did his personal best to hold the country together but it didn't do one bit of good.
   8. ☐ Fact ☒ Opinion

9. The Confederate States of America had already been organized in February of 1861, a month before Lincoln was sworn in as president.
   9. ☒ Fact ☐ Opinion

10. Poor Abraham Lincoln—what a crummy start to his presidency!
    10. ☐ Fact ☒ Opinion

---

## Away Down South In Dixie

Although many southerners disapproved of slavery, the pressure to go along with the majority who supported slavery was very strong. Many of those who thought slavery was wrong did not talk about their opinions. It was dangerous to do so!

The main reason the southern states seceded (withdrew) from the union in 1861 was because they wanted to protect their right to own slaves. They also wanted to increase the number of slaves so they could increase production of cotton and other crops that slaves tended. Many Civil War monuments in the south are dedicated to a war that was described as "just and holy."

"Dixie," a song written in 1859 that is still popular in the south, sums up the attitude of many southerners. As the song lyrics show, southerners' loyalties lay not with the union representing all the states, but with the south and the southern way of life.

**Dixie**
*I wish I was in Dixie, Hoo-ray! Hoo-ray!*
*In Dixie land I'll take my stand*
*To live and die in Dixie.*
*Away, away, away down south in Dixie!*
*Away, away, away down south in Dixie!*

(This is not the full text of the song.)

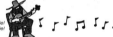

1. Why did southerners who disapproved of slavery keep their opinions to themselves?

   It was dangerous to disagree.

2. Why did southerners want more slaves?

   So they could increase production of cotton and other crops.

3. What are the words on some southern Civil War monuments?

   As "just and holy"

4. What "stand" is referred to in *Dixie*?

   ☒ stand for slavery ☐ stand against slavery ☐ stand for cotton

5. "Secede" means to

   ☐ quit ☐ fight ☒ withdraw

---

## Fact Or Opinion?

**Directions:** Read the numbered sentences and put an x in the corresponding numbered boxes to tell whether each sentence gives a fact or an opinion.

1. Dixie is a beautiful song!
   1. ☐ Fact ☒ Opinion

2. It was written in 1859 by a man named Daniel Emmett, who died in 1904.
   2. ☒ Fact ☐ Opinion

3. The song became a rallying cry for southerners because it showed where their loyalties were.
   3. ☒ Fact ☐ Opinion

4. I think their loyalty to slavery was absolutely wrong!
   4. ☐ Fact ☒ Opinion

5. These four states where people owned slaves did not secede from the union: Delaware, Maryland, Kentucky and Missouri.
   5. ☒ Fact ☐ Opinion

6. The people in these states certainly made the right moral choice.
   6. ☐ Fact ☒ Opinion

7. The ownership of one human being by another is absolutely and totally wrong under any circumstances.
   7. ☐ Fact ☒ Opinion

8. In the states that did not secede from the union, some people fought for the Union and others fought for the Confederacy of Southern States.
   8. ☒ Fact ☐ Opinion

9. Sometimes brothers fought against brothers on opposite sides of the war.
   9. ☒ Fact ☐ Opinion

10. What a horrible situation to be in!
    10. ☐ Fact ☒ Opinion

---

## Review

Although they were outnumbered, most southerners were convinced they could win the Civil War. The white population of the southern states was 5.5 million. The population was 18.9 million in the 19 states that stayed in the Union. Despite these odds, southerners felt history was on their side.

After all, the Colonists had been the underdogs against the British and had won the war for independence. Europeans also felt that Lincoln could not force the South to re-join the Union. The United Netherlands had successfully seceded from Spain. Greece had seceded from Turkey. Europeans were laying odds that two countries would take the place of what had once been the United States.

**Directions:** Answer the questions and work the puzzle.

1. What was the difference in population between the Union and Confederate states?

   13.4 million

2. The main idea is

   ✓ Although they were outnumbered, many people here and abroad felt the South would win the Civil War.

   Because they were outnumbered, the South knew winning the Civil War was a very long shot.

**Across**
4. They won the war of independence against England.
5. Did Europeans believe the South would win the war?
6. _____teen states belonged to the Union.

**Down**
1. Slaveowners lived in this area of the country.
2. The president during the Civil War.
3. To withdraw from the Union.

---

## Fun With Photography

The word photography means "writing with light." "Photo" is from the Greek word **photos** which means light. "Graphy" is from the Greek word **graphic** which means writing. Cameras don't literally write pictures of course. Instead, they imprint an image onto a piece of film.

Even the most sophisticated camera is basically a box with a piece of light sensitive film inside a box. The box has a hole at the opposite end from which the film. The light enters the box from the hole—the camera's lens—and shines on the surface of the film to create a picture. The picture that's created on the film is the image the camera's lens is pointed toward.

A **lens** is a circle of glass that is thinner at the edges and thicker in the center. The outer edges of the lens collect the light rays and draw them together at the center of the lens.

The **shutter** helps control the amount of light that enters the lens. Too much light will make the picture too light. Too little light will result in a dark picture. Electronic flash—either built into the camera or attached to the top of it—provides light when needed.

Cameras with automatic electronic flashes will provide the additional light automatically. Electronic flashes—or "flashes" as they are often called—require batteries. If your automatic flash or flash attachment quits working, a dead battery is probably the cause.

**Directions:** Answer the questions about photography.

1. From what language is the word "photography" derived?

   Greek

2. Where is the camera lens thickest?

   In the center

3. What do the outer edges of the lens do?

   They collect light

4. When is a flash needed?

   When not enough light is available

5. What does the shutter do?

   Helps control amount of light

---

## Photography Terms

Like other good professionals, photographers make their craft look easy. Their skill—like that of the graceful ice skater—comes from years of practice. Where skaters develop a sense of balance, photographers develop an "eye" for pictures. They can make important technical decisions about a photographing, or "shooting," a particular scene in the twinkling of an eye.

It's interesting to know some of the technical language that professional photographers use. "Angle of view" refers to the angle from which a photograph is taken. "Depth of field" is the distance between the nearest point and the farthest point in a photo that is in focus.

"Filling the frame" refers to the amount of space the object being photographed takes up in the picture. A close-up picture of a dog, flower or person would fill the frame. A far-away picture would not.

"ASA" refers to the speed of different types of films. "Speed" means the film's sensitivity to light. The letters ASA stand for the American Standards Association. Film manufacturers give their films ratings of 200ASA, 400ASA, etc. to indicate film speed. The higher the number on the film, the higher its sensitivity to light and the faster its speed. The faster its speed, the better it will be at clearly capturing sports images and other action shots.

**Directions:** Answer the questions about photography terms.

1. Name another term for photographing. Shooting

2. This is the distance between the nearest point and the farthest point of a photo that's in focus. Depth of field

3. This refers to the speed of different types of film. ASA rating

4. A close-up picture of someone's face would

   ☐ provide depth of field ☐ create an ASA ☒ fill the frame

5. To photograph a swimming child, which film speed is better?

   ☐ 200ASA ☒ 400ASA

## Photography Puzzler

**Directions:** Use the facts you have learned about photography to work the puzzle.

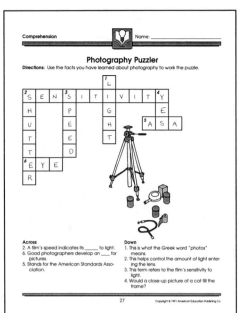

Crossword:
- Across 2: SENSITIVITY
- 5: ASA
- 6: EYE
- Down words: L (1), SHUTTER, SPEED, LIGHT, YE

**Across**

2. A film's speed indicates its _____ to light.
6. Good photographers develop an ___ for pictures.
5. Stands for the American Standards Association.

**Down**

1. This is what the Greek word "photos" means.
2. This helps control the amount of light entering the lens.
3. This term refers to the film's sensitivity to light.
4. Would a close-up picture of a cat fill the frame?

---

## Camera Care

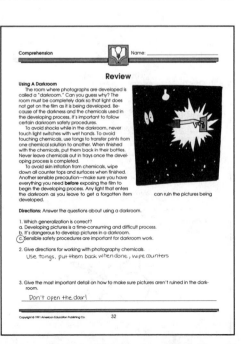

Camera dealers say many amateur photographers should take better care of their cameras. Too often, people carelessly leave expensive cameras laying out where young children or pets can get hold of them. They fail to keep put cameras back into the carrying cases that protect them. They take them to the beach and leave them laying in the sand. Another way people ruin their cameras is by leaving them for days inside a hot car.

Because they must carry so many attachments, professional photographers keep their cameras inside a large, soft shoulder bag. The bag provides extra protection for the camera, which is also protected by its camera case.

Inside the bag are compartments for film, extra lenses and other attachments. Other equipment inside a professional photographer's bag may include the following: lens hood, cable release, filters and holder, cleaning cloth and screw driver. A photographer's bag is filled with all sorts of interesting things!

Flashlights, pens, tape and sometimes a sandwich for lunch may fill out the odd assortment of objects. In addition, many photographers carry a tripod to set the camera on for still pictures. Can you see why photographers usually develop strong arm and shoulder muscles?

**Directions:** Answer the questions about caring for and storing cameras.

1. Name four ways people abuse their cameras.

1. _Leave them out_    2. _don't use case_
3. _leave them out on beach_    4. _leave them in hot car_

2. What do professional photographers carry their equipment in?

_A large soft shoulder bag_

3. Which of the following is **not** in a photographer's bag?

☐ lens hood    ☑ tripod    ☐ lens filters

4. Photographers often develop which set of muscles?

☐ legs and feet    ☑ arms and shoulders    ☐ head and neck

---

## Photographing Animals

Animals are a favorite subject of many young photographers. Cats, dogs, hamsters and other pets top the list, followed by zoo animals and the occasional lizard.

Because it's hard to get them to sit still and "perform on command," many professional photographers joke that—given a choice—they will refuse to photograph pets or small children. There **are** ways around the problem of short attention spans, however.

One way to get an appealing portrait of a cat or dog is to hold a biscuit or treat above the camera. The animal's longing look toward the food will be captured by the camera as a soulful gaze. Because it's above the camera—out of the camera's range—the treat won't appear in the picture. When you show the picture to your friends afterwards they will be impressed by your pet's loving expression.

If you are using fast film, you can take some good, quick shots of pets by simply snapping a picture right after calling their names. You'll get a different expression from your pet using this technique. Depending on your pet's disposition, the picture will capture an inquisitive expression or possibly a look of annoyance—especially if you've awakened Rover from a nap!

To photograph zoo animals, put the camera as close to the animal's cage as possible so you can shoot between the bars or wire mesh. Wild animals don't respond the same way as pets—after all, they don't know you!—so you will have to be more patient to capture a good shot. If it's legal to feed the animals, you can get their attention by having a friend toss them treats as you concentrate on shooting some good pictures.

**Directions:** Answer the questions about photographing animals.

1. Why do some professionals dislike photographing animals? _Because of animals' short attention spans_

2. What speed film should you use to photograph quick-moving pets? _Fast film_

3. To capture a pet's loving expression, hold this out of camera range. _Treat_

4. For a good picture of zoo animals

☑ get close to the cage    ☐ stand back from the cage

5. To get a zoo animal's attention, who should toss them treats?

☐ the photographer    ☑ a friend    ☐ a zoo keeper

---

## Generalization

**Directions:** Read each passage and circle the valid generalization.

1. Professional photographers know it's important to keep their cameras clean and in good working order. Amateur photographers should make sure theirs are, too. However, to take good care of your equipment, you must first understand the equipment. Camera shop owners say at least half the "defective" cameras people bring in simply need to have the battery changed!

a. Cameras are delicate and require constant care so they will work properly.
b. Many problems amateurs have are caused by lack of familiarity with their equipment.
c. Amateur photographers don't know how their cameras work.

2. Once a year, some people take their cameras to a shop to be cleaned. Most never have them cleaned at all! Those who know how can clean their cameras themselves. To avoid scratching the lens, they should use the special cloths and tissues professionals rely on. Amateurs are warned never to unloosen screws, bolts or nuts inside the camera.

a. The majority of amateur photographers never bother to have their cameras cleaned.
b. Cleaning can be tricky and should be left to professionals.
c. It's hard to find the special cleaning cloths professionals use.

3. Another simple tip from professionals—make sure your camera works **before** you take it on vacation. They suggest taking an entire roll of film and having it developed before your trip. That way, if necessary, you'll have time to have the lens cleaned or other repairs made.

a. Check out your camera beforehand to make sure it's in good working order before you travel.
b. Vacation pictures are often disappointing because the camera needs repairing.
c. Take at least one roll of film along on every vacation.

---

## Generalization

A generalization is a statement of principle that applies in many different situations.

**Directions:** Read each passage and circle the valid generalization.

1. Most people can quickly be taught to use a simple camera. However, it takes time, talent and a good eye to learn to take professional quality photographs. Patience is another quality that good photographers must possess. Those who photograph nature often will wait hours to get just the right light or shadow in their pictures.

a. There's no one who can't learn to use a camera.
b. Any patient person can become a good photographer.
c. Good photographers have a good eye for pictures.

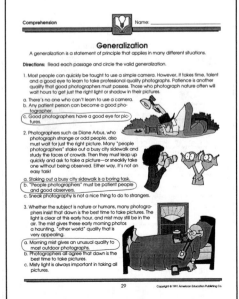

2. Photographers such as Diane Arbus, who photograph strange or odd people, also must wait for just the right picture. Many "people photographers" stake out a busy city sidewalk and study the faces of crowds. Then they must leap up quickly and ask to take a picture—or sneakily take one without being observed. Either way, it's not an easy task!

a. Staking out a busy city sidewalk is a boring task.
b. "People photographers" must be patient people and good observers.
c. Sneak photography is not a nice thing to do to strangers.

3. Whether the subject is nature or humans, many photographers insist that dawn is the best time to take pictures. The light is clear at this early hour, and mist may still be in the air. The mist gives these early morning photos a haunting, "other world" quality that is very appealing.

a. Morning mist gives an unusual quality to most outdoor photographs.
b. Photographers all agree that dawn is the best time to take pictures.
c. Misty light is always important in taking all pictures.

---

## Review

**Using A Darkroom**

The room where photographs are developed is called a "darkroom." Can you guess why? The room must be completely dark so that light does not get on the film as it is being developed. Because of the darkness and the chemicals used in the developing process, it's important to follow certain darkroom safety procedures.

To avoid shocks while in the darkroom, never touch light switches with wet hands. To avoid touching chemicals, use tongs to transfer prints from one chemical solution to another. When finished with the chemicals, put them back in their bottles. Never leave chemicals out in trays once the developing process is completed.

To avoid skin irritation from chemicals, wipe down all counter tops and surfaces when finished. Another sensible precaution—make sure you have everything you need **before** exposing the film to begin the developing process. Any light that enters the darkroom as you leave to get a forgotten item can ruin the pictures being developed.

**Directions:** Answer the questions about using a darkroom.

1. Which generalization is correct?
a. Developing pictures is a time-consuming and difficult process.
b. It's dangerous to develop pictures in a darkroom.
c. Sensible safety procedures are important for darkroom work.

2. Give directions for working with photography chemicals.
_Use tongs, put them back when done, wipe counters_

3. Give the most important detail on how to make sure pictures aren't ruined in the darkroom.
_Don't open the door!_

## Tiny Dinosaurs

When most people think of dinosaurs, they visualize enormous creatures. Actually, there were many species of small dinosaurs—some were only the size of chickens.

Like the larger dinosaurs, the Latin names of the smaller ones usually describe the creature. A small but fast species of dinosaur was **Saltopus**, which means "leaping foot." An adult **Saltopus** weighed only about two pounds (1 kilogram) and grew to be approximately two feet long. Fossils of this dinosaur, which lived about 200 million years ago, have been found only in Scotland.

Another small dinosaur with an interesting name was **Compsognathus**, which means "pretty jaw." About the same length as the **Saltopus**, the **Compsognathus** weighed about three times more. It's unlikely that these two species knew one another, since **Compsognathus** remains have been found only in France and Germany.

A small dinosaur whose remains have been found in southern Africa is **Lesothosaurus**, which means "Lesotho lizard." This lizard-like dinosaur was named only partly for its appearance. The first half of its name is based on the place its remains were found—Lesotho, in southern Africa.

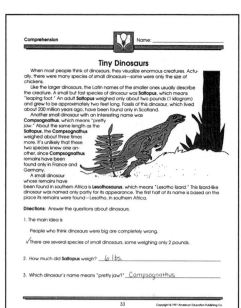

**Directions:** Answer the questions about dinosaurs.

1. The main idea is

    People who think dinosaurs were big are completely wrong.

    √ There are several species of small dinosaurs, some weighing only 2 pounds.

2. How much did **Saltopus** weigh? _6 lbs._

3. Which dinosaur's name means "pretty jaw?" _Compsognathus_

---

## Tyrannosaurus Rex

The largest meat eating animal ever to roam the earth was **Tyrannosaurus Rex**. **Rex** is Latin for "king" and, because of his size, **Tyrannosaurus** certainly was at the top of the dinosaur heap. With a length of 46 feet and a weight of 7 tons, there's no doubt this fellow commanded respect!

Unlike the smaller dinosaurs, **Tyrannosaurus** wasn't tremendously fast on his huge feet. But he could tool along at a walking speed of two to three miles an hour. Not bad, considering **Ty** was pulling along a body that weighed 14,000 pounds! Like other dinosaurs, **Tyrannosaurus** walked upright, probably balancing his 16 foot long head by lifting his massive tail.

Compared to the rest of his body, **Tyrannosaurus's** front claws were tiny. Scientists aren't really sure what the claws were for, although it seems likely that they may have been used for holding food. In that case, **Ty** would have had to lower his massive head down to his short claws to take anything in his mouth. Maybe he just used the claws to scratch nearby itches!

Because of their low metabolisms, dinosaurs did not require a lot of food for survival. Scientists speculate the **Tyrannosaurus** ate off the same huge piece of meat—usually the carcass of another dinosaur—for several weeks. What do you suppose **Tyrannosaurus** did the rest of the time?

**Directions:** Answer the questions about **Tyrannosaurus**.

1. Why was this dinosaur called **Rex**? _Rex means "king" in Latin and he was the biggest dinosaur_

2. What might **Tyrannosaurus** have used claws for? _To eat or scratch with_

3. How long was **Tyrannosaurus**? _46 feet_

4. **Tyrannosaurus** weighed

  ☐ 10,000 lbs.   ☐ 12,000 lbs.   ☑ 14,000 lbs.

5. **Tyrannosaurus** ate

  ☐ plants   ☑ other dinosaurs   ☐ birds

---

## Some Dinosaur History

Dinosaurs are so popular today that it's hard to imagine that this was not always the case. The fact is, no one had a clue that dinosaurs ever existed until about 150 years ago.

In 1841 a British scientist named Richard Owen coined the term **Dinosauria** to describe several sets of recently-discovered large fossil bones. **Dinosauria** is Latin for "terrible lizards." Like lizards, dinosaurs were reptiles. All reptiles share these characteristics: they are cold-blooded, have scaly skin, and their young hatch from eggs.

Dinosaurs were very different from reptiles in other ways. Most reptiles either have no legs—such as snakes—or have short legs set at the sides of their bodies. Crocodiles are a type of reptile with this kind of body. In contrast, most dinosaurs had fairly long legs that extended straight down from beneath their bodies. Because of their long legs, many dinosaurs were able to move fast—much faster than crocodiles and some of the other reptiles.

The balance displayed by dinosaurs was also amazing. Because their bodies are close to the ground, snakes, crocodiles and other "slithering" reptiles don't need good balance. Long-legged dinosaurs, such as the **Iguanodon**, needed balance to walk upright.

The **Iguanodon** walked on its long hind legs and used its stubby front legs as arms. On the end of its arms were five hoof-like fingers, one of which functioned as a thumb. Because it had no front teeth for tearing meat, scientists believe the **Iguanodon** was a plant-eater. Its large, flat back teeth were useful for grinding tender plants before swallowing them.

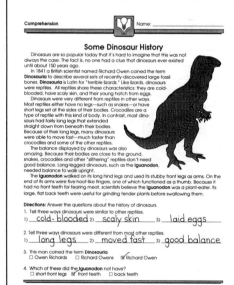

**Directions:** Answer the questions about the history of dinosaurs.

1. Tell three ways dinosaurs were similar to other reptiles.
1) _cold-blooded_ 2) _scaly skin_ 3) _laid eggs_

2. Tell three ways dinosaurs were different from most other reptiles.
1) _long legs_ 2) _moved fast_ 3) _good balance_

3. This man coined the term **Dinosauria**.
  ☐ Owen Richards   ☐ Richard Owens   ☑ Richard Owen

4. Which of these did the **Iguanodon** not have?
  ☐ short front legs   ☑ front teeth   ☐ back teeth

---

## Generalization

**Directions:** Read each passage and circle the valid generalization.

Not surprisingly, **Tyrannosaurus** had huge teeth in its mammoth head. They were six inches long! Because he was a meat-eater, **Tyrannosaurus's** teeth were sharp. They looked like spikes! In comparison, the long-necked plant-eating **Mamenchisaurus** had a tiny head and small flat teeth.

a. Scientists can't figure out why some dinosaurs had huge teeth.
(b.) **Tyrannosaurus** was probably scarier-looking than **Mamenchisaurus**.
c. Sharp teeth would have helped **Mamenchisaurus** chew better.

Dinosaurs' names often reflect their size or some other physical trait. For example, **Compsognathus** means "pretty jaw." **Saltopus** means "leaping foot." **Lesothosaurus** means "lizard."

a. Of the three species, **Lesothosaurus** was probably the fastest dinosaur.
b. Of the three species, **Compsognathus** was probably the fastest.
(c.) Of the three species, **Saltopus** was probably the fastest.

**Edmontosaurus**, a huge, three-ton dinosaur, had a thousand teeth! The teeth were cemented into chewing pads in the back of **Edmontosaurus's** mouth. Unlike the sharp teeth of the meat-eating **Tyrannosaurus**, this dinosaur's teeth were flat.

(a.) **Edmontosaurus** did not eat meat.
b. **Edmontosaurus** did not eat plants.
c. **Edmontosaurus** moved very fast.

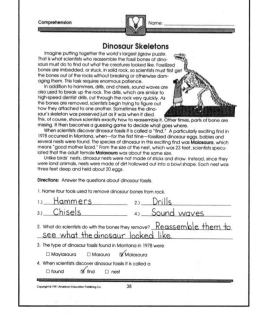

---

## Puzzling Out Dinosaurs

**Directions:** Use the facts you have learned about dinosaurs to work the puzzle.

(crossword puzzle)

Answers in grid: IGUANODON, PLANT, EGGS, HIND, SHORT, POPULAR, LIZARD, SNAKE, LEGS

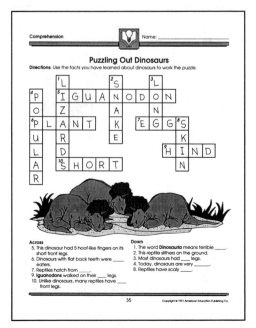

**Across**
5. This dinosaur had 5 hoof-like fingers on its short front legs.
6. Dinosaurs with flat back teeth were ____ eaters.
7. Reptiles hatch from ____.
9. **Iguanodons** walked on their ____ legs.
10. Unlike dinosaurs, many reptiles have ____ front legs.

**Down**
1. The word **Dinosauria** means terrible ____.
2. This reptile slithers on the ground.
3. Most dinosaurs had ____ legs.
4. Today, dinosaurs are very ____.
8. Reptiles have scaly ____.

---

## Dinosaur Skeletons

Imagine putting together the world's largest jigsaw puzzle. That is what scientists who reassemble the fossil bones of dinosaurs must do to find out what the creatures looked like. Fossilized bones are imbedded, or stuck, in solid rock, so scientists must first get the bones out of the rocks without breaking or otherwise damaging them. This task requires enormous patience.

In addition to hammers, drills, and chisels, sound waves are also used to break up the rock. The drills, which are similar to high-speed dentist drills, cut through the rock very quickly. As the bones are removed, scientists begin trying to figure out how they attached to one another. Sometimes the dinosaur's skeleton was preserved just as it was when it died. This, of course, shows scientists exactly how to reassemble it. Other times, parts of bone are missing. It then becomes a guessing game to decide what goes where.

When scientists discover dinosaur fossils it is called a "find." A particularly exciting find in 1978 occurred in Montana, when—for the first time—fossilized dinosaur eggs, babies and several nests were found. The species of dinosaur in this exciting find was **Maiasaura**, which means "good mother lizard." From the size of the nest, which was 23 feet, scientists speculated that the adult female **Maiasaura** was about the same size.

Unlike birds' nests, dinosaur nests were not made of sticks and straw. Instead, since they were land animals, nests were made of dirt hollowed out into a bowl shape. Each nest was three feet deep and held about 20 eggs.

**Directions:** Answer the questions about dinosaur fossils.

1. Name four tools used to remove dinosaur bones from rock.
1) _Hammers_ 2) _Drills_
3) _Chisels_ 4) _Sound waves_

2. What do scientists do with the bones they remove? _Reassemble them to see what the dinosaur looked like._

3. The type of dinosaur fossils found in Montana in 1978 was
  ☐ Mayiasaura   ☐ Masaura   ☑ Maiasaura

4. When scientists discover dinosaur fossils it is called a
  ☐ found   ☑ find   ☐ nest

Name: _____

## Generalization

**Directions:** Read each passage and circle the valid generalization.

All the plant-eating dinosaurs belonged to a common species called **Sauropods.** Most **Sauropods** were very large. They had peg-shaped teeth and they searched for food in herds. They used their long necks to reach the top branches of trees, where the most tender leaves grew.

(a) Their size, teeth and long necks made **Sauropods** perfectly suited to their environment.
b. The **Sauropods'** peg-like teeth were not well-suited to the food they ate.
c. Vegetarian dinosaurs needed short necks and sharp teeth to survive.

**Sauropods** were not the only dinosaurs that traveled in herds. Sets of different-sized fossilized dinosaur footprints discovered in Texas show that other types of dinosaurs also traveled together. The footprints—23 sets of them—were of another plant-eating dinosaur, the **Apatosaurus.**

a. All dinosaurs traveled in herds because they needed companionship.
(b) It appears that some plant-eating dinosaurs traveled in herds.
c. Traveling in herds offered dinosaurs protection and friendship.

Not all plant-eating dinosaurs were huge. The **Hypsilophodon** was only about six-and-a-half feet tall. It stood on its two back legs, and because of its smaller size, probably ran away from danger.

a. The **Hypsilophodon** didn't stand a chance against bigger dinosaurs.
(b) The **Hypsilophodon** could not eat from the tops of tall trees.
c. The **Hypsilophodon** was cowardly and always ran from danger.

---

Name: _____

## The British National Anthem

The tune to "God Save the King" is that of a folk song dating back nearly five centuries. The American song "My Country 'Tis of Thee" is sung to the same tune. The author of the words to Great Britain's unofficial national anthem is unknown. Historians say the words became popular in the middle of the 18th century, when "God Save the King" was sung in theatres throughout London. Today, because Elizabeth is queen, it is sung as "God Save the Queen."

**God Save the King**

God save our gracious King, long live our noble King
God save the King! Send him victorious, happy and glorious,
Long to reign over us,
God save the King!

O Lord and God arise. Scatter his enemies
And make them fall. Confound their politics,
Frustrate their knavish tricks. On thee our hopes we fix
God save the King.

Thy choicest gifts in store, on him be pleased to pour
Long may he reign! May he defend our laws
And ever give us cause to sing with heart and voice
God save the King!

**Directions:** Answer the questions about "God Save the King."

1. In verse one, name three major things the song asks God to do for the king.
   1.) Save him (his soul)   2.) let him live long   3.) make his reign a long one

2. In the second verse, what is wished for the king's enemies?
   That they are defeated (they scatter and fall).

3. In verse two, on whom do the people pin their hopes?
   ☐ King   ☑ God   ☐ themselves

4. In verse three, whom do the people want to defend their laws?
   ☑ King   ☐ God   ☐ themselves

---

Name: _____

## Review

Some scientists refer to dinosaurs' fossilized tracks as "footprints in time." The tracks that survived in Texas for 120 million years had been made in sand or mud. The large footprints discovered in Texas were of the **Apatosaurus.** The footprints were more than three feet across!

Although **Apatosaurus** had a long heavy tail, there is no sign that the tail hit the ground along with the feet. Scientists speculate that the place where the tracks were found was once a river bed and that the **Apatosaurus's** tails floated in the water and thus left no tracks. Another theory is that the dinosaur always carried its tail out behind it. This second theory is not as popular because scientists say it's unlikely the dinosaur would consistently carry its long heavy tail off the ground. When **Apatosaurus** rested, for example, the tail would have left its mark.

Besides Texas, fossilized tracks have been found in England, Canada, Australia and Brazil. Some tracks have also been found in New England. The tracks discovered in Canada were quite a find! They showed a pattern made by 10 species of dinosaurs. In all, about 1,700 fossilized footprints were discovered. Maybe the scientists uncovered what millions of years ago was a dinosaur playground!

**Directions:** Answer the questions about dinosaur tracks.
1. The main idea is
   ✓ Fossilized dinosaur tracks provide scientists with information from which to draw conclusions about dinosaurs' sizes and behaviors.

   Fossilized dinosaur tracks are not very useful because so few have been found in the United States.

2. Give directions on how a dinosaur might have crossed a river without its tail leaving a track.  Its tail floated in the water and left no marks on the river bed.

3. Name five countries where dinosaur tracks have been found.
   1) United States   2) Canada   3) England
   4) Australia   5) Brazil

4. Circle the valid generalization about dinosaur tracks.
   a. The fact that 10 species of tracks were found together proves dinosaurs were friends with others outside their groups.
   (b) The fact that 10 species of tracks were found together means the dinosaurs probably had gathered in that spot for water or food.
   c. The fact that 10 species of tracks were found together proves nothing!

---

Name: _____

## Puzzling Out National Anthems

**Directions:** Use the facts you have learned about the American and British national anthems to work the puzzle.

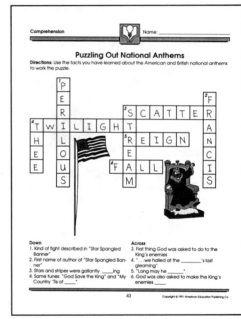

Crossword answers:
Down 1: PERILOUS
Down 2: FRANCIS
Across 3: SCATTER
Across 4: TWILIGHT
Across 5: REIGN
Across 6: FALL
(with THEE and STREM intersecting)

**Down**
1. Kind of fight described in "Star Spangled Banner"
2. First name of author of "Star Spangled Banner"
3. Stars and stripes were gallantly _____ing
4. Same tunes: "God Save the King" and "My Country 'Tis of _____."

**Across**
3. First thing God was asked to do to the King's enemies
4. ". . . we hailed at the _____'s last gleaming"
5. "Long may he _____."
6. God was also asked to make the King's enemies _____

---

Name: _____

## Our National Anthem

Written in 1814 by Francis Scott Key, our American national anthem is stirring, beautiful—and difficult to sing. Key wrote the song from aboard a ship off the coast of Maryland where one long night he watched the gunfire from a British attack on America's Fort McHenry. He was moved to write the "Star Spangled Banner" the following morning when, to his great joy, he saw that the American flag still flew over the fort—a sign that the Americans had not lost the battle.

**The Star Spangled Banner**

Oh, say can you see, by the dawn's early light
What so proudly we hailed at the twilight's last gleaming?
Whose broad stripes and bright stars, through the perilous fight
O'er ramparts we watched were so gallantly streaming?
And the rockets' red glare, the bombs bursting in air,
Gave proof through the night that our flag was still there.
Oh say does that star-spangled banner yet wave
O'er the land of the free and the home of the brave.

On the shores dimly seen through the mist of the deep,
Where the foe's haughty host in dread silence reposes,
What is that which the breeze, o'er the towering steep,
As it fitfully blows, half conceals, half discloses?
Now it catches the gleam of the morning's first beam,
In full glory reflected, now shines on the stream.
'Tis the star-spangled banner! Oh long may it wave
O'er the land of the free and the home of the brave.

**Directions:** Answer the questions about the first two verses of "The Star Spangled Banner."

1. Who wrote the "Star Spangled Banner?" Francis Scott Key

2. What is the "Star Spangled Banner?" The American flag, the song about the flag

3. In what year was the song written? 1814

4. At what time of day was the song written? Early morning

5. Tell what is meant by "The rockets' red glare, the bombs bursting in air/Gave proof through the night that our flag was still there." The light from gunfire showed the flag was still flying

6. Tell what is meant by "Now it catches the gleam of the morning's first beam." The flag gleamed in the sun's first morning rays.

---

Name: _____

## The French National Anthem

"La Marseillaise" (mar-sa-yez), the French National Anthem, was written in 1792 by army officer Rouget de Lisle during the French Revolution. After the Revolution was won, de Lisle refused to swear allegiance to the new constitution and was put in prison.

**La Marseillaise**

Ye sons of France, awake to glory!
Hark! Hark! the people bid you rise.
Your children, wives and grand-sires hoary
Behold their tears and hear their cries!
Behold their tears and hear their cries!
Shall hateful tyrants, mischief breeding,
With hireling hosts a ruffian band
Affright and desolate the land
While peace and liberty lie bleeding?

To arms, to arms ye brave!
Thy venging sword unsheath!
March on! March on! All hearts resolved.
On liberty or death.

**Directions:** Answer the questions about "La Marseillaise."

1. Use a dictionary to define "hoary." Old

2. Use a dictionary to define "ruffian." Brutal, lawless person

3. Use a dictionary to define "hireling." Person paid to do a job

4. Use a dictionary to define "unsheath." To take out

5. Whose cries were not to be heard?
   ☐ children   ☑ soldiers   ☐ wives

6. Who bids those hearing the song to fight for France?
   ☐ the children   ☐ God   ☑ the people

# The Great Wall Of China

*Built 300 years before the birth of Christ, the Great Wall in northern China was designed as a 1,500 mile long defense against invaders. Its height varies from 15 to 30 feet and its width from 12-20 feet. Photographs from space clearly show this incredible achievement of the ancient Chinese people. "Song of the Great Wall" is an ancient folk song that still rings true. China has often experienced "evil days."*

**Song of the Great Wall**

Great Wall, stretching mile on mile,
Out beyond thee lies our home.
Beans in blossom, ripening grain
Over heavens a shining dome.

Since the evil days have come
Death and murder fill the land
Children scattered, parents killed
More than human hearts can stand.

Day and night we long for home
While our bosoms swell with rage
At all costs we'll fight our way,
Fearing not what foes engage.

Great Wall, stretching mile on mile,
We will build another wall,
Of the faith of banded men,
All for one and one for all.

**Directions:** Answer the questions about the Great Wall of China.

1. How long is the Great Wall? 1,500 miles

2. In what part of China is it located? Northern China

3. When was it built? 300 years before Christ.

4. What happened to parents and children
   during the evil days? Parents killed, children scattered.

5. What "other wall" does the song
   speak of building? A wall of faith among men banding together.

---

# Song Of The Concentration Camps

*Even in the worst circumstances, songs often have had the power to lift spirits and help keep hope alive. "The Peat Bog Soldiers" was first sung in Dachau, one of Hitler's concentration camps for Jews during World War II. The job of the prisoners was—under the stern eyes of Nazi guards—to dig peat, a type of plant that was burned and used as fuel.*

**The Peat Bog Soldiers**

Far and wide as the eye can wander
Heath and bog are everywhere
Not a bird sings out to cheer us,
Oaks are standing gaunt and bare.

We are the peat bog soldiers,
We're marching with our spades to the bog.

Up and down the guards are pacing
No one, no one can go through
Flight would be a sure death facing
Guns and barbed wire begin to view.

But for us there's no complaining,
Winter will in time be past.
One day we shall cry, rejoicing,
Homeland, dear, you're mine at last.

Then will the peat bog soldiers
March no more with their spades to the bog.

**Directions:** Answer the questions about "The Peat Bog Soldiers."

1. What was peat used for? Fuel

2. Why will the prisoners be glad when winter is past? Peat won't be needed for fuel, they won't be out in the cold.

3. What would happen if prisoners tried to escape? They'd be killed.

4. The "Homeland" referred to in this poem is
   ☐ America   ☑ Germany   ☐ Russia

5. What do they not see in the bog?
   ☐ guns   ☑ birds   ☐ barbed wire

---

# Civil War Marching Song

*When soldiers march they sometimes sing a song to help them keep in step. One of the most famous marching songs of the Civil War was "The Battle Hymn of the Republic" written in 1861 by Julia Ward Howe. Mrs. Howe wrote the song after visiting a Union army camp in the North. The words are about how God is on the side of the soldiers.*

**Battle Hymn of the Republic**

Mine eyes have seen the glory of the coming of the Lord
He is trampling out the vintage where the grapes of wrath are stored
He has loosed the fateful lightning of his terrible swift sword
His truth is marching on.

Glory, glory hallelujah! Glory, glory hallelujah!
Glory, glory hallelujah! His truth is marching on.

I have seen him in the watchfires of a hundred circling camps
I have builded him an altar in the evening dews and damps
: can read his righteous sentence by the dim and flaring lamps,
His day is marching on.

Glory, glory hallelujah! Glory, glory hallelujah!
Glory, glory hallelujah! His truth is marching on.

**Directions:** Answer the questions about the "Battle Hymn of the Republic."

1. Who wrote the "Battle Hymn of the Republic?" Julia Ward Howe

2. When was the song written? 1861

3. What war was in progress at the time? Civil War

4. Why did soldiers sing while they marched? To help them keep in step.

5. What marches on along with the soldiers? God's truth

6. What did the soldiers sing about building in the evening? Altar

---

# Review

National anthems, work songs and marching songs share some common characteristics. Perhaps the most important characteristic is that the words strike an emotional response in singers and listeners alike.

Have you ever sung "The Star Spangled Banner" at a baseball game or other large public event? The next time you do, look around a bit as you sing. You will see that Americans from all walks of life and all races sing the song proudly. The words to the national anthem help create a feeling of unity among people who may not have anything else in common. The same is true of the national anthems of France, England and other countries.

Another characteristic of these types of songs is that the words are simple, the message is clear and the tune should be easy to carry. This is not always true, of course. Many people's voices crack during the high notes of "The Star Spangled Banner." But attempts to change the national anthem to "America the Beautiful" or another song with a simpler tune have always met with dismal failure. It may be hard to sing, but most Americans wouldn't trade it for any other tune. It's a long-held American tradition and nearly everyone knows the words. Americans love what this song stands for. They are proud to live in a country that is the "land of the free."

**Directions:** Answer the questions about the characteristics of national anthems, work songs and marching songs.

1. Give directions for what goes into writing a good national anthem.
   Write something that strikes a response, write simple words, clear message, easy tune

2. What does our national anthem help do?
   Create a feeling of unity among Americans

3. What happened each time someone tried to change the national anthem to "America the Beautiful" or another song? All attempts failed

4. Why do people stick with "The Star Spangled Banner" as our national anthem?
   Because it's a tradition, people know the words, they love what the song stands for

---

# Wrestling Around The World

In many countries wrestling is an honored sport. In Iceland, wrestling was called **glima**, in Switzerland it was called **schweitzer schwingen** and in Ireland it was called **cumberland**. In Japan, a form of wrestling called **sumo** began 23 centuries before the birth of Christ.

**Sumo** wrestling is still popular in Japan today. The wrestlers wear the traditional **sumo** costume of a loincloth—a piece of cloth draped across the hips and bottom—and nothing else. **Sumo** wrestlers are big men—their average weight is about 300 pounds. Wrestlers compete in small rings with sand floors. The object of the match is to push the opponent out of the ring.

However, even in the wrestling ring the Japanese are astonishingly polite. If one wrestler begins to push the other out of the ring, his opponent may shout "**Matta!**" **Matta** is Japanese for "not yet." At this point, the action stops and the wrestlers step out of the ring to take a break. Some wrestling matches in Japan must take a long, long time to complete!

1. What is wrestling called in Switzerland? Schweitzer schwingen

2. In what country is wrestling called **cumberland**? Ireland

3. What is wrestling called in Iceland? Glima

4. In what country is wrestling called **sumo**? Japan

5. How much does an average **sumo** wrestler weigh? 300 lbs

6. What does **matta** mean in Japanese? Not yet

7. What happens if a wrestler shouts **matta**! The wrestlers take a break

---

# Tennis Anyone?

Historians say a form of tennis was played outdoors in England in the 16th century. In France, the game had a much, much earlier start. "Court tennis"—named such because royal courts of kings played it—was played indoors about 1000 A.D. Six hundred years later indoor tennis was still in full swing. Records show there were 2,500 indoor courts in France at that time.

French tennis players and spectators took the game seriously. In 1780, the surgeon general of the French army recommended the game as one good for the lungs and throat. Why? Because of all the loud screaming and shouting that accompanied French games!

The word "tennis" comes from the French term **tenir** which means "take heed" or "watch out." That's what French yelled out centuries ago when they used huge rackets to whocked balls over a sagging net. Later when the game was adopted in England, **tenir** became "tennis."

Tennis is said to have come to America by way of the island of Bermuda. A young American girl, Mary Outerbridge, played the game when visiting Bermuda in 1873. She brought tennis racquets, balls and a net home to New York with her. The strange equipment puzzled customs officials—government employees who check travelers' bags to make sure they are not smuggling drugs or other substances. They reluctantly permitted Miss Outerbridge to bring the weird game to America, where it has flourished ever since!

**Directions:** Answer the questions about tennis.

1. In what year were there 2,500 indoor tennis courts in France? 1600 A.D.

2. In 1780 who recommended tennis as good for the lungs and throat?
   Surgeon general of the French Army

3. What does the French word **tenir** mean? Take heed / watch out

4. In what state was tennis first played in America? New York

5. The person who brought tennis to America was
   ☐ Marlene Outbridge   ☐ Mary Outbridge   ☑ Mary Outerbridge

# Generalization

**Direction:** Read each passage and circle the valid generalization.

Good tennis players know that footwork—where they place their feet—is vitally important to the game. When hitting a backhand stroke, face the left sideline and have the right foot set closer to the net. When hitting a forehand stroke, face the right sideline and place the left foot closer to the net.

- a. Fancy footwork is the most important factor in playing good tennis.
- (b.) Feet are placed in different positions depending on the stroke.
- c. For forehand strokes, put the right foot closer to the net.

How the racket is grasped, or gripped, is also important. You must hold it firmly enough so that it does not fly out of your hand. Yet you must not hold it stiffly, and you need to vary your grip. The grip for the forehand stroke, for example, is to place the fingers along the outside of the handle with the thumb around the inside. The heel of the palm should touch the rubber or metal grip at the bottom of the handle.

- (a.) As with footwork, different grips are required for different strokes.
- b. Always keep the heel of the palm close to the top of the racket.
- c. A good grip is more important than fancy footwork.

People who can afford to build their own tennis courts should have them laid out north and south. This way, the sunshine comes in from the sides and is not directly in the eyes of either player. Good drainage is also important, so that water is not left standing on the court after a hard rain.

- a. It's important to keep sunshine to a minimum in tennis games.
- (b.) A well laid out and properly drained court is important.
- c. Standing water on a tennis court can be swept off.

---

# Some Boxing History

The first known boxers were the ancient Greeks, who "toughened up" young men by making them box with bare fists. Later, a length of leather was wrapped around their hands and forearms to protect them. Although the sport was and is brutal, in ancient Greece boxers who killed their opponents received a stiff punishment.

During the Middle Ages—from 500 to 1500 A.D.—boxing fell out of favor. It became popular in England about a hundred years later, when the new middle class had the time and money for sports. Boxers would travel to matches held at inns and bars, and their loyal fans would follow. No gloves were used in the early 1600s in England. Instead, like the ancient Greeks, boxers used bare fists and—something new—wrestling holds. Carrier pigeons with messages tied to their bodies were trained to take news of the fights back to the boxers' home towns.

Because so many people were badly hurt or killed, padded boxing gloves began to be used in the United States around 1880. Boxing became fashionable—and safer. Harvard University offered boxing as an intramural sport in the 1880s. U.S. President Theodore Roosevelt's love of the sport helped to further popularize it. It's said that Roosevelt boxed regularly with a former heavyweight champion named Mike Donovan.

During World War I, boxing was part of the required training for army recruits. The Golden Gloves championship matches for boys, which began in the 1930s, also helped spread the sport's popularity.

1. During what period did boxing fall out of favor? _Middle Ages_

2. What university offered boxing as a sport in the 1880s? _Harvard_

3. Which U.S. president enjoyed boxing? _Theodore Roosevelt_

4. In England in the 1600s, news about boxing was sent via
- ☐ telegrams  ☑ carrier pigeons  ☐ messengers

5. The Golden Gloves championships were first offered
- ☑ in the 1930s  ☐ during World War I  ☐ during World War II

---

# Bowling Is A Ball

Like tennis and boxing, bowling is also a very old sport. It began in Germany about nine centuries ago. Bowling was first played outdoors with wooden pins and a bowling ball made from a rounded rock. And you thought modern bowling balls were heavy!

The first players were church members who bowled with Catholic bishops and priests. Those who bowled a good game were said to be blessed. Obviously, they were leading good lives. Those who bowled poorly were believed to be sinners who should clean up their acts to improve their games! The name of the game in 11th century Germany was **Kegelspiel.**

By the late 19th century, bowling was the most popular sport in Germany. A common expression for a person who had died was that he was "bowled out."

The game was introduced to America by way of Holland, where the Dutch had learned bowling from the Germans. Some Dutch citizens brought the game to Manhattan Island in 1623. The first bowling alley—outdoors, of course—opened in New York City more than 100 years later in 1732. Today, bowling is one of the most popular American sports. People who have never put on boxing gloves or raised a tennis racquet have, at one time or another, lifted and rolled a bowling ball.

**Directions:** Answer the questions about bowling.

1. The main idea is
- ✓ Bowling is a very old and a very popular sport.
- ___ Bad bowlers are sinners who should clean up their acts.

2. Who brought bowling to the United State? _Dutch citizens_

3. What was bowling called in Germany? _Kegelspiel_

4. What were the first bowling balls made from? _Rocks_

---

# Facts About Football

Like tennis courts, football fields are usually laid out in a north-south fashion so the sun doesn't shine directly into one team's eyes. The field is 120 yards long and 53 1/3 yards wide, with pairs of goal posts at each end that are at least 20 feet high.

Regulation size footballs are 11 inches long and must weigh at least 14 ounces. The object of the game is for one team of 11 to score more points than the opposing team. There are four ways to score points in football.

A touchdown, worth six points, is scored by carrying the ball across the opponent's goal line or by completing a forward pass in the opponent's end zone. When a team makes a touchdown it gets the chance to make one or two extra points via a play executed from the three-yard line. A field goal, worth three points, is made by kicking the ball from the field over the crossbar of the opponent's goal. A way to earn two points is though a play called a safety.

Football games are 60 minutes long and are divided into four quarters of 15 minutes each. Because of all the commercials and instant replays, televised games seem much longer. For college games, the halftime shows also take a lot of time.

Traditionally, college football games are played on Saturday afternoons and high school games are played on Friday nights. During the season, professional games are televised several nights a week, as well as on weekend afternoons!

**Directions:** Answer the questions about football.

1. How long is a regulation football? _11 inches_

2. How long is a football field? _120 yards_

3. How many players are on a football team? _11 players_

4. A field goal is worth
- ☐ 1 point  ☐ 2 points  ☑ 3 points

5. A touchdown is worth
- ☐ 2 points  ☐ 3 points  ☑ 6 points

---

# A Perfect Softball Pitch

Good softball pitchers make their skill look effortless and graceful. In fact, there are very specific things softball pitchers must do before, during and after they throw the ball.

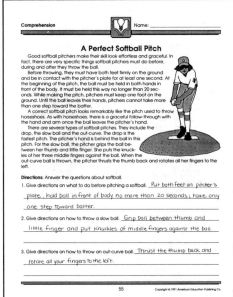

Before throwing, they must have both feet firmly on the ground and in contact with the pitcher's plate for at least one second. At the beginning of the pitch, the ball must be held in both hands in front of the body. It must be held this way no longer than 20 seconds. While making the pitch, pitchers must keep one foot on the ground. Until the ball leaves their hands, pitchers cannot take more than one step toward the batter.

A correct softball pitch looks remarkably like the pitch used to throw horseshoes. As with horseshoes, there is a graceful follow-through with the hand and arm once the ball leaves the pitcher's hand.

There are several types of softball pitches. They include the drop, the slow ball and the out-curve. The drop is the fastest pitch. The pitcher's hand is behind the ball in this pitch. For the slow ball, the pitcher grips the ball between her thumb and little finger. She puts the knuckles of her three middle fingers against the ball. When the out-curve ball is thrown, the pitcher thrusts the thumb back and rotates all her fingers to the left.

**Directions:** Answer the questions about softball.

1. Give directions on what to do before pitching a softball. _Put both feet on pitcher's plate, hold ball in front of body no more than 20 seconds; take only one step toward batter._

2. Give directions on how to throw a slow ball. _Grip ball between thumb and little finger and put knuckles of middle fingers against the ball._

3. Give directions on how to throw an out-curve ball. _Thrust the thumb back and rotate all your fingers to the left._

---

# Review

Volleyball began in Italy during the Middle Ages and was introduced to Germany in 1893. Germans called the sport **faustball.** Two years later, an American physical education teacher named William Morgan made some changes in **faustball** and brought the new game to America as "mintonette."

In **faustball,** the ball was permitted to bounce twice before being hit back over the net. In mintonette, as in modern volleyball, no bounces were allowed. Shortly after Morgan introduced the game, the director of a YMCA convinced him to change the name to something easier to pronounce. To "volley" a ball means to keep it in the air, and that's what volleyball players try to do.

A volleyball court is 60 feet long by 30 feet wide. It's divided in half (or any width) long by the width of the net. There are six players on each team, standing three by three across on each side of the net. The server is the person who begins play by hitting the ball over the net with one hand. The server stands in the back right corner of the court. Players rotate positions so each player gets a turn to serve the ball. Each team gets a maximum of three hits to return the ball over the net. If the serve is not returned, the team that served gets the point.

The most popular serve is the underhand. The server stands with the left foot forward, right knee bent, weight on the right foot. She leans slightly forward. The ball is in the partly extended left hand. The server strikes the ball off the left hand with the right hand. (Left-handers use their opposite hands.) The first team to get 15 points wins the game.

**Directions:** Answer the questions about volleyball.

1. The main idea is
- ___ Volleyball is a sport that requires a lot of strength.
- ✓ Volleyball is a simple game with 6 players on opposing sides.

2. A valid generalization about volleyball is
- (a.) It's safe, requires little equipment, and can be played by all ages.
- b. It's dangerous, difficult to learn, and appeals only to children.
- c. It's dull, slow, and takes players a long time to earn 16 points.

3. Give directions on how to deliver an underhand serve. _Put left foot forward, bend right knee, put weight on right foot. Lean forward toward ball in left hand, strike the ball off with right hand._

4. What was volleyball called in Germany? _Faustball_

## Comparing 'Word Jobs'

**Directions:** Read each paragraph, then answer the questions about making comparisons about where words come from.

The study of the origin of words is called "etymology." It's a fascinating job. To track how a word got its start, etymologists trace a word's source back as far as possible in its own language. From there, they go further back to its source in earlier languages. A "lexicographer," on the other hand, is a person who compiles words, their definitions and other facts about the words and puts them in a dictionary. The most famous U.S. lexicographer was Noah Webster, who lived between the years 1758 and 1843.

1. Compare the tasks of a lexicographer and an etymologist.

_Lexicographer prepares dictionaries; etymologist traces the origins of words_

Dictionaries do include information about the origins of words, of course. The information is supplied to lexicographers by etymologists. For example, if you look up the word "weasel" in a dictionary, you will see—in addition to its correct spelling and definition—information about where the word came from. The Old English word for weasel was **wesle**. It comes from the Latin root **weis**, which means "to flow out." The "flowing out" has to do with the horrible odor weasels are capable of making. The word "weasel" really makes a lot of sense!

2. Compare the Old English spelling of weasel to the modern spelling. What extra letter is added in the modern spelling, and what words are transposed (put in different places)?

_A is added. The LE in Old English is transposed to EL in_
_modern spelling_

3. Look up a word of your choice in a dictionary and write a paragraph about its etymology.

_____
_____
_____
_____
_____

---

## Word Detectives

Etymologists—the people who study the origin of words—really are detectives. What they seek is truth. The word stems from the Greek word **etymon**, which means "true sense." Scholars say that all languages date back to a very primitive unwritten language that etymologists call Indo-European.

Many modern languages, especially English, have incorporated untranslated foreign words into the common language. **Laissez faire** (leh-zay fair), a French word that means "let them do as they please" is often used to describe government trade policies. **Lame** (lah-may), a French word for a silvery or golden cloth, is a common fashion term.

French is not the only language Americans have taken a shine to. Here are some other words Americans have borrowed and kept from other countries. From Germany: **kindergarten, dumb, hoodulum, bagel, pretzel** and **delicatessen**. From Holland: **cookies, snoop, coleslaw, bedspreads** and **crullers**. From Spain: **tomato, avocado, coyote** and **chocolate**. From Africa: **jazz, yam, okra** and **gumbo**. From Italy: **pizza, macaroni, spaghetti** and **mafia**.

Americans have not only incorporated a lot of foreign words into the culture, they have also incorporated a love of wonderful food as well!

**Directions:** Answer the questions about the etymology of words.

1. To what primitive unwritten language does all language date?

_Indo-European_

2. What French word means a silvery or golden cloth?

_Lame_

3. From what country does **hoodulum** come from?

☒ Germany ☐ Africa ☐ Spain

4. From what country does **gumbo** come from?

☐ Germany ☒ Africa ☐ Spain

5. From what country does **snoop** come from?

☐ Germany ☐ Spain ☒ Holland

6. From what country does **dumb** come from?

☒ Germany ☐ Spain ☐ France

---

## The Name Game

Do you know the origin of your family's last name? It's fascinating to learn where family names—called "surnames"—come from.

Many names stem from occupations. Baker, Weaver, Butcher and Carpenter are examples of names that reflect the occupations once held by ancestors. Less obvious occupationally related names are Collier, which is a medieval word for "coal man," and Cooper, Long ago, men called coopers made barrels and tubs. In Middle English, cooper was spelled "couper." and collier was spelled "colyer." Colliers were coal miners.

Many occupational names are German in origin. Schmidt was the German occupation of ironsmith—a man who worked with iron. Schulz is German for "judge." Kramer is German for "small shopkeeper." Kaufman is German for "merchant."

The family name Coward, as in the late English actor Noel Coward, came from the occupation "cow-herd." Cow-herds were people in charge of herding cows. Another interesting surname of English origin is Hayward or Heyward. Long ago, when people spoke Old English, men called "hege-weards" were in charge of guarding the hedges, or fences, around property. They were in charge of keeping cows and other animals out—just in case the cow-herd didn't do a good enough job!

**Directions:** Answer the questions about the origin of surnames.

1. People with which name used to make barrels and tubs? _Cooper_

2. What are the Old English words for people who guarded hedges? _hege-weards_

3. Which country did the name "Schulz" come from? _Germany_

4. Which is not a German name?

☐ Kaufman ☐ Kramer ☒ Collier

5. Which family name refers to coal mining?

☐ Kaufman ☐ Kramer ☒ Collier

---

## Comparing Word Origins

**Directions:** Read each paragraph, then answer the questions about making comparisons about where words come from.

The etymologies of the names of diseases and vaccines is an interesting thing to know about. The etymology of the word "penicillin" is an obvious one. Penicillin, an antibiotic used to treat infections, comes from a fungus called **penicillium**. Penicillium is a Latin term meaning "pencil-like." The shape of the fungus from which penicillin is derived is shaped like—you guessed it!—a pencil.

1. Compare the spellings of the antibiotic and the fungus. How are the word endings different?

_Penicillin ends in "in"; penicillium ends in "ium."_

Anthrax is a deadly cattle disease that can be spread to man. It is characterized by black sores. The name "anthrax" comes from the Middle English word **antrax** which means "virulent ulcer." The Greek meaning of the word is "burning coal."

2. Compare the Greek meaning and the Middle English meaning of the word anthrax. Which meaning refers to what the disease is? Which refers to what it feels and looks like?

_Middle English - what disease is, Greek - what it feels and looks like_

3. Think of some other diseases you would like to know more about. Use the dictionary to look up their etymologies. Write your answers here.

_____
_____
_____
_____
_____
_____

---

## Comparing Word Origins

**Directions:** Read each paragraph, then answer the questions about making comparisons about where words come from.

Just as many surnames are related to occupations, the names of many animals are related to what they do or what they look like. The word "bear," for example, comes from a very old English word that means "the brown one." The word "raccoon" comes from an Algonquin Indian word, **drakun**, which means "the scratcher."

1. Compare the origins of the words "bear" and "raccoon." Which is based on what the animal does and which on what the animal looks like?

_Bear - what animal looks like; Raccoon - what animal does._

The cuckoo is a creature whose name reflects the sound it makes. Spelled "cou cou" in Middle English, the cuckoo is a bird that named itself! The Puffin is another bird whose name is well-chosen. From the Middle English word **poffin**, the Puffin is named because of its round, puffy shape.

2. Compare the origins of cuckoo and puffin. Which name is based on what the bird looks like and which on how the bird sounds?

_Puffin - looks, cuckoo - sound._

Orangutan is another interesting word. The word for this human-looking ape comes from a Malaysian words **oran** (man) and **utan** (forest). Together, the words mean "man of the forest." This is a good description of the animal found in the forests of Borneo and Sumatra. The origin of "monkey" is also interesting. It comes from the French word **mona** (ape) and the German **ke** (kin). Together, the words mean "kin of the ape."

3. Compare the origins of orangutan and monkey. Which name has a root word meaning "man" and which has a root word mean "ape?"

_Man - orangutan, ape - monkey._

---

## Review

Here's a quick and interesting rundown on some common words:

○ **The saxophone** was named after its inventor, Adolphe Sax, who created it in 1840.

○ **The teddy bear** was named after President Theodore Roosevelt, whose nickname was "Teddy."

○ **Moon** is based on the Middle English word **mone** which comes from an older Greek word meaning "month."

○ **Spider** comes from a Middle English word, **spithre**, which means "to spin." That's exactly what spiders do to make their webs!

○ **Pigeon** comes from an ancient French word, **pijon**, which means "peeping." That's one of the things pigeons do!

○ **Cradle** comes from a Middle English word, **cradel**, which means "little basket." That word didn't change much over the years.

**Directions:** Answer the questions about where the common words came from.

1. Which word originally meant "peeping"? _Pigeon_

2. Who was the saxophone named after? _Adolphe Sax_

3. What is the Middle English word for spider? _Spithre_

4. Who was the Teddy Bear named after? _President Theodore Roosevelt_

5. Compare the origins of moon and spider. What do they have in common?

_Both come from Middle English_

6. Compare the origins of saxophone and teddy bear. What do they have in common?

_Both were named after people_

# The MASTER SKILLS SERIES

*Workbooks for all the basic skills children need to succeed!*

### Master English

Grades K-6

### Master Math

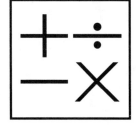

Grades K-6

### Master Reading

Grades K-6

### Master Comprehension

Grades 1-6

### Master Study Skills

Grades 1-6

### Master Spelling & Writing

Grades 1-6

**Grade K workbooks include 30 lessons plus answer key.**
**Grades 1-6 workbooks include 62 lessons plus answer key.**

# NOTES

# NOTES

# NOTES

# END OF ANSWER KEY

Dear Friend:

**A**merican Education Publishing is dedicated to designing and developing the highest quality learning materials at the most affordable prices.

The cornerstone of our efforts is a commitment to children and their need for the highest quality education in a competitive world. Our children are the primary asset in America's future. We must provide them with the skills to enrich our proud heritage.

We view the profession of teaching and the responsibility of parenting with the greatest esteem. To ensure that all children experience successful learning requires the involvement and cooperation of home, school, business and the entire community.

It is the objective of American Education Publishing to provide the educational materials and help foster an environment in which students:

✎ Start school and each grade level prepared and ready to learn.

✎ Consistently improve their skill levels in challenging subject matter.

✎ Value and respect the education process and increase their desire for learning.

✎ Gain a level of preparedness for responsible citizenship, further learning and world competition.

Thank you for your dedication to young people.

Name: _____

# Generalization

**Directions:** Read each passage and circle the valid generalization.

1. Professional photographers know it's important to keep their cameras clean and in good working order. Amateur photographers should make sure theirs are, too. However, to take good care of your camera, you must first understand the equipment. Camera shop owners say at least half the "defective" cameras people bring in simply need to have the battery changed!

   a. Cameras are delicate and require constant care so they will work properly.
   b. Many problems amateurs have are caused by lack of familiarity with their equipment.
   c. Amateur photographers don't know how their cameras work.

2. Once a year, some people take their cameras to a shop to be cleaned. Most never have them cleaned at all! Those who know how can clean their cameras themselves. To avoid scratching the lens, they should use the special cloths and tissues professionals rely on. Amateurs are warned never to unloosen screws, bolts or nuts inside the camera.

   a. The majority of amateur photographers never bother to have their cameras cleaned.
   b. Cleaning a camera can be tricky and should be left to professionals.
   c. It's hard to find the special cleaning cloths professionals use.

3. Another simple tip from professionals—make sure your camera works **before** you take it on vacation. They suggest taking an entire roll of film and having it developed before your trip. That way, if necessary, you'll have time to have the lens cleaned or other repairs made.

   a. Check out your camera beforehand to make sure it's in good working order before you travel.
   b. Vacation pictures are often disappointing because the camera needs repairing.
   c. Take at least one roll of film along on every vacation.

# Review

**Using A Darkroom**

The room where photographs are developed is called a "darkroom." Can you guess why? The room must be completely dark so that light does not get on the film as it is being developed. Because of the darkness and the chemicals used in the developing process, it's important to follow certain darkroom safety procedures.

To avoid shocks while in the darkroom, never touch light switches with wet hands. To avoid touching chemicals, use tongs to transfer prints from one chemical solution to another. When finished with the chemicals, put them back in their bottles. Never leave chemicals out in trays once the developing process is completed.

To avoid skin irritation from chemicals, wipe down all counter tops and surfaces when finished. Another sensible precaution—make sure you have everything you need **before** exposing the film to begin the developing process. Any light that enters the darkroom as you leave to get a forgotten item

can ruin the pictures being developed.

**Directions:** Answer the questions about using a darkroom.

1. Which generalization is correct?
a. Developing pictures is a time-consuming and difficult process.
b. It's dangerous to develop pictures in a darkroom.
c. Sensible safety procedures are important for darkroom work.

2. Give directions for working with photography chemicals.



3. Give the most important detail on how to make sure pictures aren't ruined in the darkroom.

# Tiny Dinosaurs

When most people think of dinosaurs, they visualize enormous creatures. Actually, there were many species of small dinosaurs—some were only the size of chickens.

Like the larger dinosaurs, the Latin names of the smaller ones usually describe the creature. A small but fast species of dinosaur was **Saltopus**, which means "leaping foot." An adult **Saltopus** weighed only about two pounds (1 kilogram) and grew to be approximately two feet long. Fossils of this dinosaur, which lived about 200 million years ago, have been found only in Scotland.

Another small dinosaur with an interesting name was **Compsognathus**, which means "pretty jaw." About the same length as the **Saltopus**, the **Compsognathus** weighed about three times more. It's unlikely that these two species knew one another, since **Compsognathus** remains have been found only in France and Germany.

A small dinosaur whose remains have been found in southern Africa is **Lesothosaurus**, which means "Lesotho lizard." This lizard-like dinosaur was named only partly for its appearance. The first half of its name is based on the place its remains were found—Lesotho, in southern Africa.

**Directions:** Answer the questions about dinosaurs.

1. The main idea is

    People who think dinosaurs were big are completely wrong.

    There are several species of small dinosaurs, some weighing only 2 pounds.

2. How much did **Saltopus** weigh? _____

3. Which dinosaur's name means "pretty jaw?" _____

# Some Dinosaur History

Dinosaurs are so popular today that it's hard to imagine that this was not always the case. The fact is, no one had a clue that dinosaurs ever existed until about 150 years ago.

In 1841 a British scientist named Richard Owen coined the term **Dinosauria** to describe several sets of recently-discovered large fossil bones. **Dinosauria** is Latin for "terrible lizards." Like lizards, dinosaurs were reptiles. All reptiles share these characteristics: they are cold-blooded, have scaly skin, and their young hatch from eggs.

Dinosaurs were very different from reptiles in other ways. Most reptiles either have no legs—such as snakes—or have short legs set at the sides of their bodies. Crocodiles are a type of reptile with this kind of body. In contrast, most dinosaurs had fairly long legs that extended straight down from beneath their bodies. Because of their long legs, many dinosaurs were able to move fast—much faster than crocodiles and some of the other reptiles.

The balance displayed by dinosaurs was also amazing. Because their bodies are close to the ground, snakes, crocodiles and other "slithering" reptiles don't need good balance. Long-legged dinosaurs, such as the **Iguanodon**, needed balance to walk upright.

The **Iguanodon** walked on its long hind legs and used its stubby front legs as arms. On the end of its arms were five hoof-like fingers, one of which functioned as a thumb. Because it had no front teeth for tearing meat, scientists believe the **Iguanodon** was a plant-eater. Its large, flat back teeth were useful for grinding tender plants before swallowing them.

**Directions:** Answer the questions about the history of dinosaurs.

1. Tell three ways dinosaurs were similar to other reptiles.

1) _____ 2) _____ 3) _____

2. Tell three ways dinosaurs were different from most other reptiles.

1) _____ 2) _____ 3) _____

3. This man coined the term **Dinosauria**.
   ☐ Owen Richards   ☐ Richard Owens   ☐ Richard Owen

4. Which of these did the **Iguanodon** not have?
   ☐ short front legs   ☐ front teeth   ☐ back teeth

Name: _____

# Puzzling Out Dinosaurs

**Directions:** Use the facts you have learned about dinosaurs to work the puzzle.

## Across

5. This dinosaur had 5 hoof-like fingers on its short front legs.
6. Dinosaurs with flat back teeth were _____ eaters.
7. Reptiles hatch from _____.
9. **Iguanodons** walked on their _____ legs.
10. Unlike dinosaurs, many reptiles have _____ front legs.

## Down

1. The word **Dinosauria** means terrible _____.
2. This reptile slithers on the ground.
3. Most dinosaurs had _____ legs.
4. Today, dinosaurs are very _____.
8. Reptiles have scaly _____.

# Tyrannosaurus Rex

The largest meat eating animal ever to roam the earth was **Tyrannosaurus Rex**. **Rex** is Latin for "king" and, because of his size, **Tyrannosaurus** certainly was at the top of the dinosaur heap. With a length of 46 feet and a weight of 7 tons, there's no doubt this fellow commanded respect!

Unlike the smaller dinosaurs, **Tyrannosaurus** wasn't tremendously fast on his huge feet. But he could tool along at a walking speed of two to three miles an hour. Not bad, considering **Ty** was pulling along a body that weighed 14,000 pounds! Like other dinosaurs, **Tyrannosaurus** walked upright, probably balancing his 16 foot long head by lifting his massive tail.

Compared to the rest of his body, **Tyrannosaurus's** front claws were tiny. Scientists aren't really sure what the claws were for, although it seems likely that they may have been used for holding food. In that case, **Ty** would have had to lower his massive head down to his short claws to take anything in his mouth. Maybe he just used the claws to scratch nearby itches!

Because of their low metabolisms, dinosaurs did not require a lot of food for survival. Scientists speculate the **Tyrannosaurus** ate off the same huge piece of meat—usually the carcass of another dinosaur—for several weeks. What do you suppose **Tyrannosaurus** did the rest of the time?

**Directions:** Answer the questions about **Tyrannosaurus**.

1. Why was this dinosaur called **Rex**? _____

2. What might **Tyrannosaurus** have used claws for? _____

3. How long was **Tyrannosaurus** ? _____

4. **Tyrannosaurus** weighed

   ☐ 10,000 lbs.    ☐ 12,000 lbs.    ☐ 14,000 lbs.

5. **Tyrannosaurus** ate

   ☐ plants    ☐ other dinosaurs    ☐ birds

Name: _____

# Generalization

**Directions:** Read each passage and circle the valid generalization.

Not surprisingly, **Tyrannosaurus** had huge teeth in its mammoth head. They were six inches long! Because he was a meat-eater, **Tyrannosaurus's** teeth were sharp. They looked like spikes! In comparison, the long-necked plant-eating **Mamenchisaurus** had a tiny head and small flat teeth.

a. Scientists can't figure out why some dinosaurs had huge teeth.
b. **Tyrannosaurus** was probably scarier-looking than **Mamenchisaurus**.
c. Sharp teeth would have helped **Mamenchisaurus** chew better.

Dinosaurs' names often reflect their size or some other physical trait. For example, **Compsognathus** means "pretty jaw." **Saltopus** means "leaping foot." **Lesothosaurus** means "lizard."

a. Of the three species, **Lesothosaurus** was probably the fastest dinosaur.
b. Of the three species, **Compsognathus** was probably the fastest.
c. Of the three species, **Saltopus** was probably the fastest.

**Edmontosaurus**, a huge, three-ton dinosaur, had a thousand teeth! The teeth were cemented into chewing pads in the back of **Edmontosaurus's** mouth. Unlike the sharp teeth of the meat-eating **Tyrannosaurus**, this dinosaur's teeth were flat.

a. **Edmontosaurus** did not eat meat.
b. **Edmontosaurus** did not eat plants.
c. **Edmontosaurus** moved very fast.

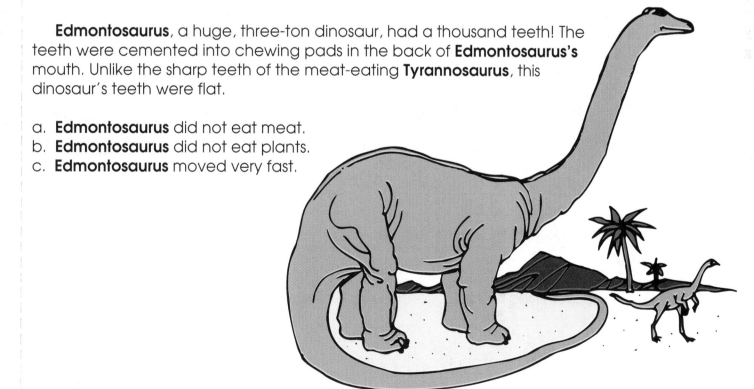

# Dinosaur Skeletons

Imagine putting together the world's largest jigsaw puzzle. That is what scientists who reassemble the fossil bones of dinosaurs must do to find out what the creatures looked like. Fossilized bones are imbedded, or stuck, in solid rock, so scientists must first get the bones out of the rocks without breaking or otherwise damaging them. This task requires enormous patience.

In addition to hammers, drills, and chisels, sound waves are also used to break up the rock. The drills, which are similar to high-speed dentist drills, cut through the rock very quickly. As the bones are removed, scientists begin trying to figure out how they attached to one another. Sometimes the dinosaur's skeleton was preserved just as it was when it died. This, of course, shows scientists exactly how to reassemble it. Other times, parts of bone are missing. It then becomes a guessing game to decide what goes where.

When scientists discover dinosaur fossils it is called a "find."  A particularly exciting find in 1978 occurred in Montana, when—for the first time—fossilized dinosaur eggs, babies and several nests were found. The species of dinosaur in this exciting find was **Maiasaura**, which means "good mother lizard." From the size of the nest, which was 23 feet, scientists speculated that the adult female **Maiasaura** was about the same size.

Unlike birds' nests, dinosaur nests were not made of sticks and straw. Instead, since they were land animals, nests were made of dirt hollowed out into a bowl shape. Each nest was three feet deep and held about 20 eggs.

**Directions:** Answer the questions about dinosaur fossils.

1. Name four tools used to remove dinosaur bones from rock.

1.) _____          2.) _____

3.) _____          4.) _____

2. What do scientists do with the bones they remove? _____

_____

3. The type of dinosaur fossils found in Montana in 1978 were

☐ Mayiasaura          ☐ Masaura          ☐ Maiasaura

4. When scientists discover dinosaur fossils it is called a

☐ found          ☐ find          ☐ nest

38

# Generalization

**Directions:** Read each passage and circle the valid generalization.

All the plant-eating dinosaurs belonged to a common species called **Sauropods**. Most **Sauropods** were very large. They had peg-shaped teeth and they searched for food in herds. They used their long necks to reach the top branches of trees, where the most tender leaves grew.

a. Their size, teeth and long necks made **Sauropods** perfectly suited to their environment.
b. The **Sauropods**' peg-like teeth were not well-suited to the food they ate.
c. Vegetarian dinosaurs needed short necks and sharp teeth to survive.

**Sauropods** were not the only dinosaurs that traveled in herds. Sets of different-sized fossilized dinosaur footprints discovered in Texas show that other types of dinosaurs also traveled together. The footprints—23 sets of them—were of another plant-eating dinosaur, the **Apatosaurus.**

a. All dinosaurs traveled in herds because they needed companionship.
b. It appears that some plant-eating dinosaurs traveled in herds.
c. Traveling in herds offered dinosaurs protection and friendship.

Not all plant-eating dinosaurs were huge. The **Hypsilophodon** was only about six-and-a-half feet tall. It stood on its two back legs and, because of its smaller size, probably ran away from danger.

a. The **Hypsilophodon** didn't stand a chance against bigger dinosaurs.
b. The **Hypsilophodon** could not eat from the tops of tall trees.
c. The **Hypsilophodon** was cowardly and always ran from danger.

Name: _____

# Review

Some scientists refer to dinosaurs' fossilized tracks as "footprints in time." The tracks that survived in Texas for 120 million years had been made in sand or mud. The large footprints discovered in Texas were of the **Apatosaurus**. The footprints were more than three feet across!

Although **Apatosaurus** had a long heavy tail, there is no sign that the tail hit the ground along with the feet. Scientists speculate that the place where the tracks were found was once a river bed and that the **Apatosaurus's** tails floated in the water and thus left no tracks. Another theory is that the dinosaur always carried its tail out behind it. This second theory is not as popular because scientists say it's unlikely the dinosaur would consistently carry its long heavy tail off the ground. When **Apatosaurus** rested, for example, the tail would have left its mark.

Besides Texas, fossilized tracks have been found in England, Canada, Australia and Brazil. Some tracks have also been found in New England. The tracks discovered in Canada were quite a find! They showed a pattern made by 10 species of dinosaurs. In all, about 1,700 fossilized footprints were discovered. Maybe the scientists uncovered what millions of years ago was a dinosaur playground!

**Directions:** Answer the questions about dinosaur tracks.

1. The main idea is

Fossilized dinosaur tracks provide scientists with information from which to draw

conclusions about dinosaurs' sizes and behaviors.

Fossilized dinosaur tracks are not very useful because so few have been found in the United States.

2. Give directions on how a dinosaur might have crossed a river without its tail leaving a

track. _____

3. Name five countries where dinosaur tracks have been found.

1) _____ 2) _____ 3) _____

4) _____ 5) _____

4. Circle the valid generalization about dinosaur tracks.
   a. The fact that 10 species of tracks were found together proves dinosaurs were friends with others outside their groups.
   b. The fact that 10 species of tracks were found together means the dinosaurs probably had gathered in that spot for water or food.
   c. The fact that 10 species of tracks were found together proves nothing!

# Our National Anthem

*Written in 1814 by Francis Scott Key, our American national anthem is stirring, beautiful—and difficult to sing. Key wrote the song from aboard a ship off the coast of Maryland where one long night he watched the gunfire from a British attack on America's Fort McHenry. He was moved to write the "Star Spangled Banner" the following morning when, to his great joy, he saw that the American flag still flew over the fort—a sign that the Americans had not lost the battle.*

**The Star Spangled Banner**

Oh, say can you see, by the dawn's early light
What so proudly we hailed at the twilight's last gleaming?
Whose broad strips and bright stars, through the perilous fight
O'er ramparts we watched were so gallantly streaming?
And the rockets' red glare, the bombs bursting in air,
Gave proof through the night that our flag was still there.
Oh say does that star-spangled banner yet wave
O'er the land of the free and the home of the brave.

On the shores dimly seen through the mist of the deep,
Where the foe's haughty host in dread silence reposes
What is that which the breeze, oe'er the towering steep,
As it fitfully blows, half conceals, half discloses?
Now it catches the gleam of the morning's first beam,
In full glory reflected, now shines on the stream.
'Tis the star-spangled banner! Oh long may it wave
O'er the land of the free and the home of the brave.

**Directions:** Answer the questions about the first two verses of "The Star Spangled Banner."

1. Who wrote the "Star Spangled Banner?" _____

2. What is the "Star Spangled Banner?" _____

3. In what year was the song written? _____

4. At what time of day was the song written? _____

5. Tell what is meant by "The rockets' red glare, the bombs bursting in air/Gave proof through

   the night that our flag was still there." _____

6. Tell what is meant by "Now it catches the gleam of the morning's first beam."

_____

# The British National Anthem

*The tune to "God Save the King" is that of a folk song dating back nearly five centuries. The American song "My Country 'Tis of Thee" is sung to the same tune. The author of the words to Great Britain's unofficial national anthem is unknown. Historians say the words became popular in the middle of the 18th century, when "God Save the King" was sung in theatres throughout London. Today, because Elizabeth is queen, it is sung as "God Save the Queen."*

**God Save the King**

God save our gracious King, long live our noble King
God save the King! Send him victorious, happy and glorious,
Long to reign over us,
God save the King!

O Lord and God arise. Scatter his enemies
And make them fall. Confound their politics,
Frustrate their knavish tricks, On thee our hopes we fix
God save the King.

Thy choicest gifts in store, on him be pleased to pour
Long may he reign! May he defend our laws
And ever give us cause to sing with heart and voice
God save the King!

**Directions:** Answer the questions about "God Save the King."

1. In verse one, name three major things the song asks God to do for the king.

1.) _____ 2.) _____ 3.) _____

2. In the second verse, what is wished for the king's enemies?

_____

3. In verse two, on whom do the people pin their hopes?

☐ King  ☐ God  ☐ themselves

4. In verse three, whom do the people want to defend their laws?

☐ King  ☐ God  ☐ themselves

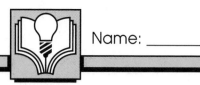

Name: _____

# Puzzling Out National Anthems

**Directions:** Use the facts you have learned about the American and British national anthems to work the puzzle.

**Down**

1. Kind of fight described in "Star Spangled Banner"
2. First name of author of "Star Spangled Banner"
3. Stars and stripes were gallantly _____ing
4. Same tunes: "God Save the King" and "My Country 'Tis of _____"

**Across**

3. First thing God was asked to do to the King's enemies
4. "...we hailed at the _____'s last gleaming"
5. "Long may he _____"
6. God was also asked to make the King's enemies _____

Name: _____

# The French National Anthem

*"La Marseillaise"* (mar-sa-yez), the French National Anthem, was written in 1792 by army officer Rouget de Lisle during the French Revolution. After the Revolution was won, de Lisle refused to swear allegiance to the new constitution and was put in prison.

**La Marseillaise**

Ye sons of France, awake to glory!
Hark! Hark! the people bid you rise.
Your children, wives and grand-sires hoary
Behold their tears and hear their cries!
Behold their tears and hear their cries!

Shall hateful tyrants, mischief breeding,
With hireling hosts a ruffian band
Affright and desolate the land
While peace and liberty lie bleeding?

To arms, to arms ye brave!
Thy venging sword unsheath!
March on! March on! All hearts resolved.
On liberty or death.

**Directions:** Answer the questions about "La Marseillaise."

1. Use a dictionary to define "hoary." _____

2. Use a dictionary to define "ruffian." _____

3. Use a dictionary to define "hireling." _____

4. Use a dictionary to define "unshealth." _____

5. Whose cries were not to be heard?

   ☐ children   ☐ soldiers   ☐ wives

6. Who bids those hearing the song to fight for France?

   ☐ the children   ☐ God   ☐ the people

Name: _____

# The Great Wall Of China

*Built 300 years before the birth of Christ, the Great Wall in northern China was designed as a 1,500 mile long defense against invaders. Its height varies from 15 to 30 feet and its width from 12-20 feet. Photographs from space clearly show this incredible achievement of the ancient Chinese people. "Song of the Great Wall" is an ancient folk song that still rings true. China has often experienced "evil days."*

**Song of the Great Wall**

Great Wall, stretching mile on mile,
Out beyond thee lies our home.
Beans in blossom, ripening grain
Over heavens a shining dome.

Since the evil days have come
Death and murder fill the land
Children scattered, parents killed
More than human hearts can stand.

Day and night we long for home
While our bosoms swell with rage
At all costs we'll fight our way,
Fearing not what foes engage.

Great Wall, stretching mile on mile,
We will build another wall,
Of the faith of banded men,
All for one and one for all.

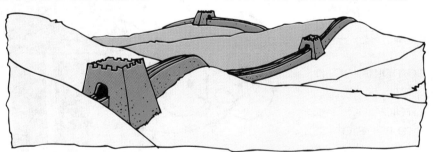

**Directions:** Answer the questions about the Great Wall of China.

1. How long is the Great Wall?_____

2. In what part of China is it located? _____

3. When was it built? _____

4. What happened to parents and children

   during the evil days? _____

5. What "other wall" does the song

   speak of building? _____

# Song Of The Concentration Camps

*Even in the worst circumstances, songs often have had the power to lift spirits and help keep hope alive. "The Peat Bog Soldiers" was first sung in Dachau, one of Hitler's concentration camps for Jews during World War II. The job of the prisoners was—under the stern eyes of Nazi guards—to dig peat, a type of plant that was burned and used as fuel.*

**The Peat Bog Soldiers**

Far and wide as the eye can wander
Heath and bog are everywhere
Not a bird sings out to cheer us,
Oaks are standing gaunt and bare.

We are the peat bog soldiers,
We're marching with our spades to the bog.

Up and down the guards are pacing
No one, no one can go through
Flight would be a sure death facing,
Guns and barbed wire greet our view.

But for us there's no complaining,
Winter will in time be past.
One day we shall cry, rejoicing,
Homeland, dear, you're mine at last.

Then will the peat bog soldiers
March no more with their spades to the bog.

**Directions:** Answer the questions about "The Peat Bog Soldiers."

1. What was peat used for? _____

2. Why will the prisoners be glad when winter is past?_____

3. What would happen if prisoners tried to escape? _____

4. The "Homeland" referred to in this poem is
   ☐ America   ☐ Germany   ☐ Russia

5. What do they not see in the bog?
   ☐ guns   ☐ birds   ☐ barbed wire

Name: _____

# Civil War Marching Song

*When soldiers march they sometimes sing a song to help them keep in step. One of the most famous marching songs of the Civil War was "The Battle Hymn of the Republic" written in 1861 by Julia Ward Howe. Mrs. Howe wrote the song after visiting a Union army camp in the North. The words are about how God is on the side of the soldiers.*

**Battle Hymn of the Republic**

Mine eyes have seen the glory of the coming of the Lord
He is trampling out the vintage where the grapes of wrath are stored
He has loosed the fateful lightning of his terrible swift sword
His truth is marching on.

Glory, glory hallelujah! Glory, glory hallelujah!
Glory, glory hallelujah! His truth is marching on.

I have seen him in the watchfires of a hundred circling camps
I have builded him an altar in the evening dews and damps
I can read his righteous sentence by the dim and flaring lamps,
His day is marching on.

Glory, glory hallelujah! Glory, glory hallelujah!
Glory, glory hallelujah! His truth is marching on.

**Directions:** Answer the questions about the "Battle Hymn of the Republic."

1. Who wrote the "Battle Hymn of the Republic?" _____

2. When was the song written? _____

3. What war was in progress at the time? _____

4. Why did soldiers sing while they marched? _____

5. What marches on along with the soldiers? _____

6. What did the soldiers sing about building in the evening?_____

# Review

National anthems, work songs and marching songs share some common characteristics. Perhaps the most important characteristic is that the words strike an emotional response in singers and listeners alike.

Have your ever sung "The Star Spangled Banner" at a baseball game or other large public event? The next time you do, look around a bit as you sing. You will see that Americans from all walks of life and all races sing the song proudly. The words to the national anthem help create a feeling of unity among people who may not have anything else in common. The same is true of the national anthems of France, England and other countries.

Another characteristic of these types of songs is that the words are simple, the message is clear and the tune should be easy to carry. This is not always true, of course. Many people's voices crack during the high notes of "The Star Spangled Banner." But attempts to change the national anthem to "America the Beautiful" or another song with a simpler tune have always met with dismal failure. It may be hard to sing, but most Americans wouldn't trade it for any other tune. It's a long-held American tradition and nearly everyone knows the words. Americans love what this song stands for. They are proud to live in a country that is the "land of the free."

**Directions:** Answer the questions about the characteristics of national anthems, work songs and marching songs.

1. Give directions for what goes into writing a good national anthem.

_____

2. What does our national anthem help do?

_____

3. What happened each time someone tried to change the national anthem to "America

the Beautiful" or another song? _____

4. Why do people stick with "The Star Spangled Banner" as our national anthem?

_____

Name: _____

# Wrestling Around The World

In many countries wrestling is an honored sport. In Iceland, wrestling was called **glima**, in Switzerland it was called **schweitzer schwingen** and in Ireland it was called **cumberland**. In Japan, a form of wrestling called **sumo** began 23 centuries before the birth of Christ.

**Sumo** wrestling is still popular in Japan today. The wrestlers wear the traditional **sumo** costume of a loincloth—a piece of cloth draped across the hips and bottom—and nothing else. **Sumo** wrestlers are big men—their average weight is about 300 pounds. Wrestlers compete in small rings with sand floors. The object of the match is to push the opponent out of the ring.

However, even in the wrestling ring the Japanese are astonishingly polite. If one wrestler begins to push the other out of the ring, his opponent may shout "**Matta**!" **Matta** is Japanese for "not yet." At this point, the action stops and the wrestlers step out of the ring to take a break. Some wrestling matches in Japan must take a long, long time to complete!

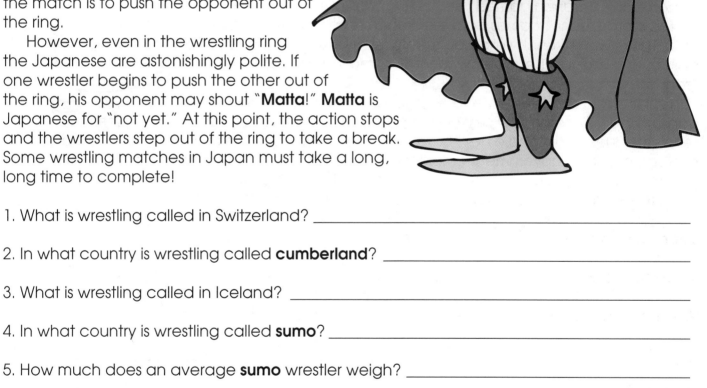

1. What is wrestling called in Switzerland? _____

2. In what country is wrestling called **cumberland**? _____

3. What is wrestling called in Iceland? _____

4. In what country is wrestling called **sumo**? _____

5. How much does an average **sumo** wrestler weigh? _____

6. What does **matta**! mean in Japanese? _____

7. What happens if a wrestler shouts **matta**! _____

# Tennis Anyone?

Historians say a form of tennis was played outdoors in England in the 16th century. In France, the game had a much, much earlier start. "Court tennis"—named such because royal courts of kings played it—was played indoors about 1000 A.D. Six hundred years later indoor tennis was still in full swing. Records show there were 2,500 indoor courts in France at that time.

French tennis players and spectators took the game seriously. In 1780, the surgeon general of the French army recommended the game as one good for the lungs and throat. Why? Because of all the loud screaming and shouting that accompanied French games!

The word "tennis" comes from the French term **tenir** which means "take heed" or "watch out." That's what French yelled out centuries ago when they used huge rackets to whacked balls over a sagging net. Later when the game was adopted in England, **tenir** became "tennis."

Tennis is said to have come to America by way of the island of Bermuda. A young American girl, Mary Outerbridge, played the game when visiting Bermuda in 1873. She brought tennis racquets, balls and a net home to New York with her. The strange equipment puzzled customs officials—government employees who check travelers' bags to make sure they are not smuggling drugs or other substances. They reluctantly permitted Miss Outerbridge to bring the weird game to America, where it has flourished ever since!

**Directions:** Answer the questions about tennis.

1. In what year were there 2,500 indoor tennis courts in France? _____

2. In 1780 who recommended tennis as good for the lungs and throat?

_____

3. What does the French word **tenir** mean? _____

4. In what state was tennis first played in America? _____

5. The person who brought tennis to America was

☐ Marlene Outbridge    ☐ Mary Outbridge    ☐ Mary Outerbridge

Name: _____

# Generalization

**Direction:** Read each passage and circle the valid generalization.

Good tennis players know that footwork—where they place their feet—is vitally important to the game. When hitting a backhand stroke, face the left sideline and have the right foot set closer to the net. When hitting a fore-hand stroke, face the right sideline and place the left foot closer to the net.

   a. Fancy footwork is the most important factor in playing good tennis.
   b. Feet are placed in different positions depending on the stroke.
   c. For forehand strokes, put the right foot be closer to the net.

How the racket is grasped, or gripped, is also important. You must hold it firmly enough so that it does not fly out of your hand. Yet you must not hold it stiffly, and you need to vary your grip. The grip for the forehand stroke, for ex-ample, is to place the fingers along the outside of the handle with the thumb around the inside. The heel of the palm should touch the rubber or metal grip at the bottom of the handle.

   a. As with footwork, different grips are required for different strokes.
   b. Always keep the heel of the palm close to the top of the racket.
   c. A good grip is more important than fancy footwork.

People who can afford to build their own tennis courts should have them laid out north and south. This way, the sunshine comes in from the sides and is not directly in the eyes of either player. Good drainage is also important, so that water is not left standing on the court after a hard rain.

   a. It's important to keep sunshine to a minimum in tennis games.
   b. A well laid out and properly drained court is important.
   c. Standing water on a tennis court can be swept off.

# Some Boxing History

The first known boxers were the ancient Greeks, who "toughened up" young men by making them box with bare fists. Later, a length of leather was wrapped around their hands and forearms to protect them. Although the sport was and is brutal, in ancient Greece boxers who killed their opponents received a stiff punishment.

During the Middle Ages—from 500 to 1500 A.D.—boxing fell out of favor. It became popular in England about a hundred years later, when the new middle class had the time and money for sports. Boxers would travel to matches held at inns and bars, and their loyal fans would follow. No gloves were used in the early 1600s in England. Instead, like the ancient Greeks, boxers used bare fists and—something new— wrestling holds. Carrier pigeons with messages tied to their bodies were trained to take news of the fights back to the boxers' home towns.

Because so many people were badly hurt or killed, padded boxing gloves began to be used in the United States around 1880. Boxing became fashionable—and safer. Harvard University offered boxing as an intramural sport in the 1880s. U.S. President Theodore Roosevelt's love of the sport helped to further popularize it. It's said that Roosevelt boxed regularly with a former heavyweight champion named Mike Donovan.

During World War I, boxing was part of the required training for army recruits. The Golden Gloves championship matches for boys, which began in the 1930s, also helped spread the sport's popularity.

1. During what period did boxing fall out of favor? _____


2. What university offered boxing as a sport in the 1880s? _____


3. Which U.S. president enjoyed boxing? _____

4. In England in the 1600s, news about boxing was sent via

   ☐ telegrams    ☐ carrier pigeons    ☐ messengers

5. The Golden Gloves championships were first offered

   ☐ in the 1930s    ☐ during World War I    ☐ during World War II

Name: _____

# Bowling Is A Ball

Like tennis and boxing, bowling is also a very old sport. It began in Germany about nine centuries ago. Bowling was first played outdoors with wooden pins and a bowling ball made from a rounded rock. And you thought modern bowling balls were heavy!

The first players were church members who bowled with Catholic bishops and priests. Those who bowled a good game were said to be blessed. Obviously, they were leading good lives. Those who bowled poorly were believed to be sinners who should clean up their acts to improve their games! The name of the game in 11th century Germany was **Kegelspiel**.

By the late 19th century, bowling was the most popular sport in Germany. A common expression for a person who had died was that he was "bowled out."

The game was introduced to America by way of Holland, where the Dutch had learned bowling from the Germans. Some Dutch citizens brought the game to Manhattan Island in 1623. The first bowling alley—outdoors, of course—opened in New York City more than 100 years later in 1732. Today bowling is one of the most popular American sports. People who have never put on boxing gloves or raised a tennis racquet have, at one time or another, lifted and rolled a bowling ball.

**Directions:** Answer the questions about bowling.

1. The main idea is

    Bowling is a very old and a very popular sport.

    Bad bowlers are sinners who should clean up their acts.

2. Who brought bowling to the United State? _____

3. What was bowling called in Germany? _____

4. What were the first bowling balls made from? _____

# Facts About Football

Like tennis courts, football fields are usually laid out in a north-south fashion so the sun doesn't shine directly into one team's eyes. The field is 120 yards long and 53 1/3 yards wide, with pairs of goal posts at each end that are at least 20 feet high.

Regulation size footballs are 11 inches long and must weigh at least 14 ounces. The object of the game is for one team of 11 to score more points than the opposing team. There are four ways to score points in football.

A touchdown, worth six points, is scored by carrying the ball across the opponent's goal line or by completing a forward pass in the opponent's end zone. When a team makes a touchdown it gets the chance to make one or two extra points via a play executed from the three-yard line. A field goal, worth three points, is made by kicking the ball from the field over the crossbar of the opponent's goal. A way to earn two points is though a play called a safety.

Football games are 60 minutes long and are divided into four quarters of 15 minutes each. Because of all the commercials and instant replays, televised games seem much longer. For college games, the halftime shows also take a lot of time.

Traditionally, college football games are played on Saturday afternoons and high school games are played on Friday nights. During the season, professional games are televised several nights a week, as well as on weekend afternoons!

**Directions:** Answer the questions about football.

1. How long is a regulation football? _____

2. How long is a football field? _____

3. How many players are on a football team? _____

4. A field goal is worth

  ☐ 1 point    ☐ 2 points    ☐ 3 points

5. A touchdown is worth

  ☐ 2 points    ☐ 3 points    ☐ 6 points

54

# A Perfect Softball Pitch

Good softball pitchers make their skill look effortless and graceful. In fact, there are very specific things softball pitchers must do before, during and after they throw the ball.

Before throwing, they must have both feet firmly on the ground and be in contact with the pitcher's plate for at least one second. At the beginning of the pitch, the ball must be held in both hands in front of the body. It must be held this way no longer than 20 seconds. While making the pitch, pitchers must keep one foot on the ground. Until the ball leaves their hands, pitchers cannot take more than one step toward the batter.

A correct softball pitch looks remarkably like the pitch used to throw horseshoes. As with horseshoes, there is a graceful follow-through with the hand and arm once the ball leaves the pitcher's hand.

There are several types of softball pitches. They include the drop, the slow ball and the out-curve. The drop is the fastest pitch. The pitcher's hand is behind the ball in this pitch. For the slow ball, the pitcher grips the ball between her thumb and little finger. She puts the knuckles of her three middle fingers against the ball. When the out-curve ball is thrown, the pitcher thrusts the thumb back and rotates all her fingers to the left.

**Directions:** Answer the questions about softball.

1. Give directions on what to do before pitching a softball. _____

_____

_____

2. Give directions on how to throw a slow ball. _____

_____

_____

3. Give directions on how to throw an out-curve ball. _____

_____

_____

# Review

Volleyball began in Italy during the Middle Ages and was introduced to Germany in 1893. Germans called the sport **faustball**. Two years later, an American physical education teacher named William Morgan made some changes in **faustball** and brought the new game to Americans as "mintonette."

In **faustball**, the ball was permitted to bounce twice before being hit back over the net. In mintonette, as in modern volleyball, no bounces were allowed. Shortly after Morgan introduced the sport, the director of a YMCA convinced him to change the name to something easier to pronounce. To "volley" a ball means to keep it in the air, and that's what volleyball players try to do.

A volleyball court is 60 feet long by 30 feet wide. It's divided in half by an eight-foot high net. There are six players on each team, standing three by three across on each side of the net. The server is the person who begins play by hitting the ball over the net with one hand. The server stands in the back right corner of the court. Players rotate positions so each player gets a turn to serve the ball. Each team gets a maximum of three hits to return the ball over the net. If the serve is not returned, the team that served gets the point.

The most popular serve is the underhand. The server stands with the left foot forward, right knee bent, weight on the right foot. She leans slightly forward. The ball is in the partly extended left hand. The server strikes the ball off the left hand with the right hand. (Left-handers use their opposite hands.) The first team to get 15 points wins the game.

**Directions:** Answer the questions about volleyball.

1. The main idea is

    Volleyball is a sport that requires a lot of strength.
    Volleyball is a simple game with 6 players on opposing sides.

2. A valid generalization about volleyball is
    a. It's safe, requires little equipment, and can be played by all ages.
    b. It's dangerous, difficult to learn, and appeals only to children.
    c. It's dull, slow, and takes players a long time to earn 16 points.

3. Give directions on how to deliver an underhand serve. _____

_____

4. What was volleyball called in Germany? _____

Name: _____

# Comparing 'Word Jobs'

**Directions:** Read each paragraph, then answer the questions about making comparisons about where words come from.

The study of the origin of words is called "etymology." It's a fascinating job. To track how a word got its start, etymologists trace a word's source back as far as possible in its own language. From there, they go further back to its source in earlier languages. A "lexicographer," on the other hand, is a person who compiles words, their definitions and other facts about the words and puts them in a dictionary. The most famous U.S. lexicographer was Noah Webster, who lived between the years 1758 and 1843.

1. Compare the tasks of a lexicographer and an etymologist.

_____

Dictionaries do include information about the origins of words, of course. The information is supplied to lexicographers by etymologists. For example, if you look up the word "weasel" in a dictionary, you will see—in addition to its correct spelling and definition—information about where the word came from. The Old English word for weasel was **wesle**. It comes from the Latin root **weis**, which means to flow out. The "flowing out" has to do with the horrible odor weasels are capable of making. The word "weasel" really makes a lot of sense!

2. Compare the Old English spelling of weasel to the modern spelling. What extra letter is added in the modern spelling, and what words are transposed (put in different places)?

_____

_____

3. Look up a word of your choice in a dictionary and write a paragraph about its etymology.

_____

_____

_____

_____

Name: _____

# The Name Game

Do you know the origin of your family's last name? It's fascinating to learn where family names—called "surnames"—come from.

Many names stem from occupations. Baker, Weaver, Butcher and Carpenter are examples of names that reflect the occupations once held by ancestors. Less obvious occupationally related names are Collier, which is a medieval word for "coal man," and Cooper. Long ago, men called coopers made barrels and tubs. In Middle English, cooper was spelled "couper," and collier was spelled "colyer." Colliers were coal miners.

Many occupational names are German in origin. Schmidt was the German occupation of ironsmith— a man who worked with iron. Schulz is German for "judge." Kramer is German for "small shop-keeper." Kaufman is German for "merchant."

The family name Coward, as in the late English actor Noel Coward, came from the occupation "cow-herd." Cow-herds were people in charge of herding cows. Another interesting surname of English origin is Hayward or Heyward. Long ago, when people spoke Old English, men called "hege-weards" were in charge of guarding the hedges, or fences, around property. They were in charge of keeping cows and other animals out—just in case the cow-herd didn't do a good enough job!

**Directions:** Answer the questions about the origin of surnames.

1. People with which name used to make barrels and tubs? _____

2. What are the Old English words for people who guarded hedges?_____

3. Which country did the name "Schulz" come from? _____

4. Which is not a German name?

    ☐ Kaufman   ☐ Kramer  ☐ Collier

5. Which family name refers to coal mining?

    ☐ Kaufman   ☐ Kramer  ☐ Collier

Name: _____

# Comparing Word Origins

**Directions:** Read each paragraph, then answer the questions about making comparisons about where words come from.

Just as many surnames are related to occupations, the names of many animals are related to what they do or what they look like. The word "bear," for example, comes from a very old English word that means "the brown one." The word "raccoon" comes from an Algonquin Indian word, **drakun**, which means "the scratcher."

WHERE DOES YOUR NAME COME FROM?

1. Compare the origins of the words "bear" and "raccoon." Which is based on what the animal does and which on what the animal looks like?

_____

The cuckoo is a creature whose name reflects the sound it makes. Spelled "*cou cou*" in Middle English, the cuckoo is a bird that named itself! The Puffin is another bird whose name is well-chosen. From the Middle English word **poffin**, the Puffin is named because of its round, puffy shape.

2. Compare the origins of cuckoo and puffin. Which name is based on what the bird looks like and which on how the bird sounds?

_____

Orangutan is another interesting word. The word for this human-looking ape comes from a Malaysian words **oran** (man) and **utan** (forest). Together, the words mean "man of the forest." This is a good description of the animal found in the forests of Borneo and Sumatra. The origin of "monkey" is also interesting. It comes from the French word **mona** (ape) and the German **ke** (kin). Together, the words mean "kin of the ape."

3. Compare the origins of orangutan and monkey. Which name has a root word meaning "man" and which has a root word mean "ape?"

_____

# Word Detectives

Etymologists—the people who study the origin of words—really are detectives. What they seek is truth. The word stems from the Greek word **etymon**, which means "true sense." Scholars say that all languages date back to a very primitive unwritten language that etymologists call Indo-European.

Many modern languages, especially English, have incorporated untranslated foreign words into the common language. **Laissez faire** (lah-zay fair), a French word that means "let them do as they please" is often used to describe government trade policies. **Lame** (lah-may), a French word for a silvery or golden cloth, is a common fashion term.

French is not the only language Americans have taken a shine to. Here are some other words Americans have borrowed and kept from other countries. From Germany: **kindergarten**, **dumb**, **hoodulum**, **bagel**, **pretzel** and **delicatessen**. From Holland: **cookies**, **snoop**, **coleslaw**, **bedspreads** and **crullers**. From Spain: **tomato**, **avocado**, **coyote** and **chocolate**. From Africa: **jazz**, **yam**, **okra** and **gumbo**. From Italy: **pizza**, **macaroni**, **spaghetti** and **mafia**.

Americans have not only incorporated a lot of foreign words into the culture, they have also incorporated a love of wonderful food as well!

**Directions:** Answer the questions about the etymology of words.

1. To what primitive unwritten language does all language date?

_____

2. What French word means a silvery or golden cloth?

_____

3. From what country does **hoodulum** come from?

☐ Germany     ☐ Africa     ☐ Spain

4. From what country does **gumbo** come from?

☐ Germany     ☐ Africa     ☐ Spain

5. From what country does **snoop** come from?

☐ Germany     ☐ Spain     ☐ Holland

6. From what country does **dumb** come from?

☐ Germany     ☐ Spain     ☐ France

Name: _____

# Comparing Word Origins

**Directions:** Read each paragraph, then answer the questions about making comparisons about where words come from.

The etymologies of the names of diseases and vaccines is an interesting thing to know about. The etymology of the word "penicillin" is an obvious one. Penicillin, an antibiotic used to treat infections, comes from a fungus called **penicillium**. **Penicillium** is a Latin term meaning "pencil-like." The shape of the fungus from which penicillin is derived is shaped like—you guessed it!—a pencil.

1. Compare the spellings of the antibiotic and the fungus. How are the word endings different?

_____

Anthrax is a deadly cattle disease that can be spread to man. It is characterized by black sores. The name "anthrax" comes from the Middle English word **antrax** which means "virulent ulcer." The Greek meaning of the word is "burning coal."

2. Compare the Greek meaning and the Middle English meaning of the word anthrax. Which meaning refers to what the disease is? Which refers to what it feels and looks like?

_____

3. Think of some other diseases you would like to know more about. Use the dictionary to look up their etymologies. Write your answers here.

_____

_____

_____

_____

_____

Name: _____

# Review

Here's a quick and interesting rundown on some common words:

o **The saxophone** was named after its inventor, Adolphe Sax, who created it in 1840.

o **The teddy bear** was named after President Theodore Roosevelt, whose nickname was "Teddy."

o **Moon** is based on the Middle English word **mone** which comes from an older Greek word meaning "month."

o **Spider** comes from a Middle English word, **spithre**, which means "to spin." That's exactly what spiders do to make their webs!

o **Pigeon** comes from an ancient French word, **pijon**, which means "peeping. That's one of the things pigeons do!

o **Cradle** comes from a Middle English word, **cradel**, which means "little basket." This word didn't change much over the years.

**Directions:** Answer the questions about where the common words came from.

1. Which word originally meant "peeping?" _____

2. Who was the saxophone named after? _____

3. What was the Middle English word for spider? _____

4. Who was the Teddy Bear named after? _____

5. Compare the origins of moon and spider. What do they have in common?

_____

6. Compare the origins of saxophone and teddy bear. What do they have in common?

_____